AGEING IN NORTH EAST INDIA
MANIPUR PERSPECTIVE

AGEING IN NORTH EAST INDIA MANIPUR PERSPECTIVE

Edited By
S. Kipgen
&
Benjamin *Nattar*

AKANSHA PUBLISHING HOUSE
NEW DELHI-110002 (INDIA)

AKANSHA PUBLISHING HOUSE
4649-B/21, Ansari Road
Darya Ganj, New Delhi - 110 002
Ph.: 23263193 / 9811582579 / 09435116718
Fax: 011-23263193
Email: ektabooks@yahoo.com

Ageing in North East India: Manipur Perspective

First Published 2009
Reprint 2026
ISBN 978-81-8370-174-7

PRINTED IN INDIA

Published by Akansha Publishing House, New Delhi and Printed at Aryan Enterprises, Delhi.

CONTENTS

FOREWORD

In the recent years, much literature on North-East India has been published by the scholars of this region on various issues related to the people and the region as a whole. However, the issues related to ageing, the elderly persons of this region are not properly addressed so far. Although every 1st October is being observed as the international day for the elderly, yet the magnitude of the problems of the elderly persons in North-East India is not properly addressed neither in the myriad seminars organized by various academic bodies and the NGO's nor their problems and aspirations are documented.

Considering the lacunae in this field, the Indian Council of Social Science Research, North Eastern Regional Centre (ICSSR-NERC), Shillong took the initiative to bridge the gap by organizing a series of State level seminars on the magnitude of the problems of the elderly persons in North-East during 2006-2008. This book has its origin in one of the seminars organized by the Manipur College Imphal, Manipur during March

2008. Dr S. Kipgen & Benjamin Nattar and colleagues in the college took the keen interest in the seminar not only in organizing it but also compiling and revising the papers presented in the seminar in the present book format.

The papers carefully put together for this volume by Dr S. Kipgen & Benjamin Nattar raise some of the vital questions related to the elderly persons in the State of Manipur and will, I am sure, prove to be essential reading for anyone interested in the field of ageing.

ICSSR-NERC
Shillong

C. J. Thomas
Director

LIST OF CONTRIBUTORS

Smt. Ch. Jamuna Devi is a Lecturer (Selection Grade) in the Department of English, Manipur College.

Dr. M. Manimohan Meitei is a Geographer in the Directorate of Census Operation, Government of Manipur, Imphal.

Dr. Th. Achouba Singh is a Professor in the Department of Community Medicine, Regional Institute of Medical Sciences (RIMS), Imphal.

Dr. R.K. Lenin is an Associate Professor in Psychiatry, RIMS, Imphal.

Shri S. Kunjabihari Singh is a Retd. IAS officer and an active member of Senior Citizens Welfare Association, Manipur.

Dr. Linus Neli, M.H.R., Ph.D. is a visiting Professor at the Oriens Theological College, Shillong, and at the Institute of Oriental Canon Law, Bangalore. Presently, he is the Vicar General of the Catholic Archdiocese of Imphal.

Dr. H. Dwijasekhar Sharma is the retired Principal of D.M. College of Science, Imphal.

Shri S. Saratkumar Sharma is the Joint Director (WCD), Social Welfare Department, Government of Manipur, Imphal.

Shri S. Benjamin Nattar, is a Lecturer (Selection Grade) in the Department of Political Science, Manipur College, Imphal.

Dr. Sheikhohao Kipgen, is a Lecturer in the Department of History in Manipur College, Imphal.

KEYNOTE ADDRESS

Ch. Jamuna Devi

Manipur College, the third oldest premier college in the State, is indeed privileged to organize and host this One-day state Level Seminar, sponsored by the Indian Council of Social Science Research – North Eastern Region Centre, Shillong and Directorate of Higher Education, Government of Manipur.

Old age is a natural life cycle of change. It is global as it is experienced by all commanded respect because they controlled the sources of power, wealth, land, political office, and the fate of their family members. However, it has been observed that there has been some changes in the society as new generations perceive a different mental outlook due to increasing pressures of urbanization, changes in occupation pattern and perhaps a change in life styles too. Today, the problems faced by the elderly are increasing all over the world. The magnitude and manifestation vary from place to place.

Even though the problems of the aged are manifold, they could broadly be categorized as

(i) Biological and physiological.

(ii) Non-availability and non-affordability of health care facilities to mitigate their illness, especially for those living in far-flung rural areas.

(iii) Nutritional problems, the lack of awareness of nutritional food.

(iv) Psychological problems like maladjustment, lack of regard, affection, love; feeling of isolation, loneliness, neglect, insecurity, humiliation and frustration, intergeneration relations and generation gap, rigidity, dissatisfaction with life.

(v) Socio-cultural problems like diffusion, change in status, disintegration of joint family system, non-participation in decision making, increasing materialism, displacement from rural to urban areas, change in values, norms etc.

Taking cognizance of the magnitude of the problem of the elderly, the UN had declared the year 1999 as the International Year of the Older Persons and October 1, as the Aged Peoples Day for celebrating and acknowledging the contribution of the older people to society. The rapid increase in population of the elderly in the world has caught the attention and concern of the United Nations. It was thought to be a concern of the developing countries but now the issue has become equally important in all the developing countries.

The problems stated here are universally noticed with local variations and characters. Even in a traditional orthodox society like Manipur, the problems of the elderly are on the rise, as the society itself is undergoing various changes. The contradiction between of traditional values and the values of modernity has aggravated the problems of the aged people. The increase in education, lack of employment opportunities in the state, a fluid law and order situation and various other factors have led to the emigration of educated youth to various parts of the country and the world. While the trend *per se* is to be appreciated, the effect on the elderly who are left to look after themselves is an unwelcome reality. Violence and violence-related activities have serious impact on the elders especially when they themselves become victims. They are highly vulnerable to attack and theft. In case of illness like stroke no one may come to their rescue in time. The aged everywhere are subject to special problems. He/she is constantly exposed to personal and emotional insecurity besides requiring to earn beyond the age of superannuation in order to survive and sustain a semblance of personal status. A sense of social isolation is strongly felt because of disjunction from work relationship, demise of relatives and friends. The situation worsens when there is physical incapacity and financial stringency. Financial problems add to the misery of the aged. Having spent all their hard earned money on their children's education and marriage, they are greatly demoralized when their offspring's refuse to give them shelter.

To mitigate the problems, various measures need to be taken up. Economic security is to be assured to them, though the problem of the elderly is more psychological than material. This is because the economic problem is associated with all stages of life. They should be provided the facility to organize themselves to fight for their rights, to chalk our strategies to solve their problems and relieve them from their loneliness. Healthcare facilities should be widespread and made functional especially in the hill areas of Manipur. Adult education programmes need to be intensified and strengthened. An educated person has more self confidence and emotional stability than an illiterate. Recreational facilities, parks, health clubs are as important as housing and income security. Extension services, radio and television programmes, regular and special classes should find a place in the welfare programme of the aged. Efforts may be made to help them organize themselves. The government should form a policy framework including special old age pensions which are adequate to cover their financial requirement. The present pension is too meager in this period of growing inflation. Proper health care facilities should be provided in government hospitals. The aged should not be neglected because the general notion is that they become hypochondriac as they grow old. Due to migration of children, the aged parents are left deserted which gives rise to multiple problems, separation itself is a major setback in their lives.

Re-deployment of retired people, voluntary services of resourceful elderly people, useful engagement of the aged in the field of writing, translating, counseling etc., will prove to be very good for them. This would minimize their feeling of anxiety, insecurity, isolation, frustration, depression and would keep them physically and mentally healthy. Children should be taught the values of respect of elders from the very beginning both at home and at school.

Taking advantage of the ICSSR sponsored seminar, it is hoped that the deliberations and suggestions of the learned resource persons and the delegates will be an eye-opener to the society, NGOs and policy makers in the state in particular and the country in general.

INTRODUCTION

S. Kipgen & Benjamin Nattar

Manipur, an erstwhile princely state, merged with Indian Union in 1949, lies in the Northeastern corner of the country. An ancient kingdom with over 2000 years of history, a home to a number of tribes and tongues, a proud and highly self-conscious people, vibrant in sports, art, culture, dance, martial arts etc., Manipur is indeed fit to be a 'jewel of India', as described by Pandit Jawaharlal Nehru, the first Prime Minister of India. The state has an area of 22,327 sq. km., with a population of 23,88,634 according to 2001 census. It is bounded by other Indian states of Nagaland, Assam, Mizoram and Myanmar (Burma). The topography of Manipur is unique, as one-tenth of the land is plain at the centre surrounded by nine-tenth of hilly land. The valley is predominantly occupied by the Meiteis most of whom are Vaishnavite Hindus, and the Meitei Pangals (Manipuri Muslims). Whereas there are 33 different tribal groups, which include the Naga and Kuki-Chin people mostly living in the hills and in the Imphal Valley of Manipur. Majority of the tribal people belongs to Christianity.

Though there is a strong racial affinity between the Meiteis and the tribals yet social and cultural divisions are clearly evident among them. The people of Manipur possess good physique and live a rather healthy life in a comparatively less polluted environment. Even though individual Manipuris have made marks in various chosen fields, Manipur today is affected by various social and political ills. Old age problem was never thought to be very serious, but latest trends show that it is time we give some serious thought to this.

In every society the aged people serve as advisors and consultants. In fact, society needs them. They should be considered as social assets, core of human capital and cultural resources rather than treating them as a social liability.

Very little study has been done so far, on the problem of the aged people in Manipur. With a view to study the problem of the aged, in March 2008, a One-Day state level seminar on 'Magnitude of the Problem of the Elderly Persons in the Northeastern Region of India with special Reference to Manipur' was organized by Manipur College, Imphal. The day-long seminar covered wide areas such as the status of the aged population in Manipur, the general health condition and health care services, biological and psychological aspects, socio-economic status, social planning and welfare schemes, policy matters etc. The Seminar was sponsored by

Indian Council of Social Science Research, North Eastern Regional Centre, Shillong, Meghalaya and also partly funded by Directorate of University and Higher Education, Government of Manipur. This book is based on revised version of the papers presented at the seminar.

The population of the elders continues to rise all over the world, and so also in India. Various factors have contributed to the growth of the elderly population. There had not been much study done on this field. In Manipur aforesaid seminar was the first of its kind to have discussed the problems of the elderly people. Manipur College provided a platform to those who were actively engaged in the elderly people's welfare to air their views and suggest measures for managing the problems of the elders. There were eight papers read in the seminar. The authors of these papers are experts drawn from different walks of life having full knowledge of the problem of the elderly. Some of the papers have been revised and form the texts of this book. We are grateful to Dr. C.J. Thomas, Director, ICSSR North Eastern Regional Centre, Shillong, for his constant reminders without which this volume would not have seen the light of its day.

In the keynote address Ch. Jamuna Devi, highlighted the features and characteristics of the aged people in general, their physical and psychological problems. She has given in a nutshell the peculiar problems being faced by the aged people in the Manipur society. To mitigate the problems of the aged some suggestions are also offered by her.

M. Manimohan Meetei in his paper on the 'Aged Population in Manipur' describes the growth of the aged people in Manipur statistically. Age statistics are very important and play a vital role as most of the analysis of population characteristics is performed according to age and sex. Even though census in Manipur was introduced in 1901, the records up to 1951 formed part of Assam. It's only from 1951, Manipur had separate census. The percentage of aged population was 8.73% in 1951 as against 6.71% in 2001, whereas the aged people in all India level constituted 7.45%. He has explained clearly statistical concepts like single age return, growth of aged population in figures and tables, distribution of aged population in Manipur, district-wise, the marital status of the aged, migration of the aged people, work and employment of aged people, distribution of scheduled castes and tribes among the aged etc. Manipur stands next to Tripura in the Northeast region in terms of elderly people. At the same time, he is of the opinion that the facilities available to aged people here, is very little. The government has not done anything for the well being of the old people.

H. Dwijasekhar Sharma in his paper on the 'Social and Economic Status of Elders: Issues and Challenges' has mentioned that due to the advent of science and technology and medical advancement, the aged population in Manipur is on the rise. This reflects greater socio-economic potential for economic growth. In a patriarchal and feudal society like Manipur, ancestor worship was a popular tradition. But the onslaught of westernization and democracy had marginalized and discarded such cultural and traditional values leading the rise of individualism and nuclear families. The foundation of all feudal and social institutions was shaken. As such in the psyche of the elders, they are unloved and uncared for. When the father is not in a position to leave a family fortune as in the case of poor or low middle income group, they consider themselves a burden to their sons. The symbiosis between father and son has also undergone a sea change among the Manipuri society.

According to the author, the material and human relationship between the father and the son has to adjust mutually under 'mutualism symbioses'. They need to gain extra holistic pleasure to make their lives livable. They also need to become positive in approach and look upon each other as real benefactors. The elders should also apply and practice cluster thinking for productive purposes even in their threshold stage of their lives. Being the core of human capital, their expertise, experience and innovation should be incentives so as to adopt the culture of cluster policy thinking. He further says that social solidarity also needs to be integrated and pro activated by both the social fabric and the state apparatus.

Linus Neli's paper on 'The Ageing Scenario among the Tribes of Manipur' is unique in its own way. This paper examines the ageing problems peculiar to more than thirty-three tribes inhabiting in Manipur and comprising about 41% of the State's total population. The people in Manipur are popularly classified into 'valley people' and 'hill people' largely due to anthropological and topographical reasons. The Meiteis and the Meitei Pangals are the main inhabitants in the valley, while the two generic groups in the hills are the Nagas and Kuki-Chin Mizos who occupy the surrounding hills of the state. Under the Constitution of India, all the Hill people of Manipur fall into the category of the Scheduled Tribes.

The hill tribes have many features quite distinct from their counterparts in the valley, the principal differences being their origin, food habits, customs, polity, religion, and living standards, thus making their social interactions and intermarriages often difficult, if not incompatible. Besides, the attention and efforts of the government do not always percolate adequately through the hills to the people due to the rugged terrain, inadequate infrastructures and social organizations. This paper critically probe into the present problems and status of the old aged people among the tribes of Manipur. This paper was based on a sample survey carried out in the hill areas of Manipur.

Saratkumar Sharma in his paper on 'Care of the Elderly – A Social Concern' highlighted the constitutional provisions for the care of the elderly. As an officer of the Directorate of Social Welfare Department, he has narrated the government's various welfare measures for the elderly, resource utilization under social security programme of state government, like payment of old age pension, funding for old age homes, and other such schemes. He further pointed out some of the measures for easing the problems of the aged in the state of Manipur.

R. K. Lenin Singh, in his paper on 'Psycho-social issues of the elderly persons in the state of Manipur' has given the various causes that may lead to the psycho-social problems of the elders. Generally more attention was paid on physical factors such as exercise, diet, sleep, genetics etc., in dealing with the problems of the elders. But evidence has suggested that psycho-social and social-economic factors also have significant influence on health and ageing. According to the author, Manipur is an elderly friendly place. But of late various problems have come up. Factors such as, retirement, grief and mourning, empty nester, migration, nuclear families, generation gap, lack of recreational facilities, financial problems, elderly abuse, law and order situation, AIDS and HIV problems, physical illness, mental health problems, dementia have aggravated the problems of the elderly people. In Manipur, old age was never seen as a social problem, as respect for the elders and obligation to the old parents always formed a part and parcel of the cultural value system of the society. But urbanization, migration of educated youth to other places have caused immense problem to the aged.

In his paper on 'The Elderly Woes and Interventions', S. Kunjabihari Singh gives his personal encounters of elderly peoples' woes in Manipur and outside. In the three cases given by him, the old people are seen on the receiving end whether they had well groomed their children or not. With advancing age, old people begin to be not liked or even disliked by their children and grandchildren as their priorities in life are different. The sons and daughters-in-law of today, with their high profile tastes of privacy and personal choice, prefer the elderly to remain shut to their domain; and stubbornly refrain from taking the parents into confidence in family and social matters. In the modern society, the elders get marginalized more than ever before. It is rather fortunate that Manipur society is an open society with a strong social bond. There is less of elderly abuse due to possible social gaze and condemnation. The author, well aware of various government acts and schemes for the elderly, gives some practical suggestions. Two major approaches are proposed; one is institutional where various public packages and schemes could be implemented. The other approach is promoting physical infrastructure like old age homes especially for those who are physically and financially not sound enough. In these ways, the problems of the elderly could be mitigated to a certain extent.

Th. Achouba's paper on 'The general health condition and access to health care service of the old aged people' is a short presentation describing the various health problems of the elders. According to the author, the major health problems of the aged people in Manipur are joint pain/ache, diabetics, cataract, hearing problems, hypertension, tooth-ache, stomach ailments etc. The elderly people have no proper health care services in the state. Besides these, the suffering of the aged people is multiplied due to problems like psycho-social, loneliness, non-availability of health care facilities.

MANIPUR

role as most of the analysis of population characteristics is performed according to age and sex. Age is usually defined in demographic literature as the number of completed years or elapsed since the birth of the individual. But it will be needed to discuss, how far the actual age data is provided for various analysis. It is not properly understood by many people that the question on determining age is extremely deceptive and not simple and state forward as it appears at first sight. The census data on age is only based the completed years of the person concerned. To determine a man's age, it has many bases as calculated from Horoscope (Kuthi) or any locally known traditional methods and the actual birth certificate issued by the competent authority like Registrar of Municipal Council, Hospital, etc. It is also found from the academic certificate or voter's list as similar or dissimilar to their actual date of birth. Whether a man is young or old is indicated by his age and not by seeing or assumption. At present, the age of superannuation of the Central Government Servant is fixed at 60 years calculating from their academic date of birth though for academician, it is 62 years but for state Government employees it vary from one state to others as below 60 years. Those persons who crossed the age of 65 years are known as "Senior Citizen" of the country. The present paper is attempted to highlight the 60 years and above as old age person i.e. "Aged Population".

Objective

The problem of ageing (becoming old) is a global problem in the sense that it is experienced by all the societies, but its magnitude and its manifestations are not the same everywhere. Proportion of aged population may be difference from place-to-place or rural to urban by its geographical location and social and cultural phenomenon. An attempt is made here to count how many aged population (60+) in different category is resided in Manipur as per 2001 Census.

Methodology

The structural framework of the present paper is based on census data. Sex and age structure for every decade is collected and published by the Census of India since 1881. A brief statistical analysis is made here based on census finding. Diagram like line graph, age pyramid and map are also presented here to highlight or focus the data.

Table 1
Manipur—Growth of Aged Population (60+), 1901-2001

Census Year	*Aged Population*	*Proportion to total Population*	*% of Growth/ variation*
1	*2*	*3*	*4*
1901	-	-	-
1911	-	-	(+) 4.8
1921	-	-	(+) 21.9
1931	-	-	(-) 1.1
1941	-	-	-
1951	5,028	8.73	-
1961	43,545	5.58	-
1971	65,328	6.09	(+) 50.0
1981	83,466	5.87	(+) 27.8
1991	111,105	6.05	(+) 33.1
2001*	145,470	6.71	(+) 30.9

Source: *Census of India, 2001*

Note: Total Aged Population is not available from 1901 to 1941 and 1951 was calculated on sample basis in 57,580 persons.

* Excluding Mao-Maram, Paomata and Purul sub-divisions of Senapati district.

What is Census: The word "Census" is derived from the **Latin** word 'Censere' meaning 'to assess' or 'to rate'. In and around $1^{st}/2^{nd}$ century BC, the magistrates in Rome were required to prepare population registers for the purpose of imposing taxes and also to determine the liability of adult males for compulsory military service. About 3,000 years BC ancient Babylonia, China and Egypt had introduced cadastral surveys.

The fall of Roman Empire and the growth of feudal system brought to an end the first phase of periodical censuses. One of the earliest completed censuses involving inhabitants of all ages was taken in German city of Nuremberg in 1449. Other provincial or municipal censuses were also conducted in Switzerland in the 15th and 16th centuries AD. Before independence of India, there were more than 700 princely ruled states in the Indian Dominion. For the purpose of military services, taxes, etc., numbers of head counting were conducted in their own efforts in the early periods, although population estimates were also obtained during the reign of Chandragupta Maurya, and during Akbar's rule. Since 1865, the preparation of the modern census was started. During 1865-72, modern Census was conducted non-synchronously. In 1872, it has been popularly known as the first population Census of India. However, the first synchronous census covered the whole of India simultaneously was held in 1881. Since then Censuses have been undertaken continuously once every ten years and the Census of India 2001 being the fourteenth and the latest in the series.

The first Manipur state Census was introduced in the year 1881 but 1891 census record was destroyed due to Anglo-Manipuri War in that year. From 1901 onwards, the population of the state had been counted without breaking once in ten years. Till 1951, the state census was included as a part of Assam Province and separated its own Directorate since 1961 census.

Single Age Return: While collecting the age data in both sexes, most of the common people preferred their ages either in '0' ending or '5' ending number. For example, a man's actual age is supposed to be either 69 or 71, he may prefer to 70, similarly 85 for either 84 or 86. In another case, preference will be given to even number than odd number, say instead of 91 or 93, he may report as 92. It can be seen clearly that in 1991, of the total 111,105 aged population in the state, 61.78 per cent are recorded by different 6 age groups together, i.e. 26.49 per cent belonged to 60 years of age alone, 12.52 per cent at 65 years, 12.40 per cent at 70 years, 4.62 per cent at 75 years, 4.51 per cent at 80 years and 1.24 per cent at 85 years and other age groups together recorded 38.22 per cent only. Similar trends were also repeated in 2001 as 60 years (19.39%), 65 years (12.20 %), 70 years (12.33%), 75 years (5.15 %), 80 years (4.37 %) and 85 years (1.24 %) but it is little increased in other ages together (45.32 %) (Fig. I).

Growth of Aged Population

The United Nations is looking forward to focus the problems and prospects of the aged population and also highlighted the rapid growth of its population so that they recognized the International Day of Older Persons in the year 1990. According to Census, the aged population (60+) of India has increased from 5.63 per cent in 1961 to 6.58 in 1991 and again to 7.45 per cent in 2001.

Table 2
Manipur—Aged Population (60+) in Five Year, 2001

State/District	*Age-Group*					
	Total	*60-64*	*65-69*	*70-74*	*75-79*	*80+*
1	*2*	*3*	*4*	*5*	*6*	*7*
Manipur*	145,470	48,133	35,897	28,806	15,459	17,175
Senapati	8,417	3,170	2,175	1,525	752	795
Tamenglong	6,363	2,139	1,446	1,192	667	919
Churachandpur	14,002	4,977	3,547	2,660	1,266	1,552
Bishnupur	15,427	4,918	3,721	3,094	1,701	1,993
Thoubal	24,038	7,923	6,172	4,752	2,555	2,636
Imphal West	34,342	10,748	8,172	7,064	3,936	4,422
Imphal East	27,153	8,814	6,672	5,473	2,966	3,228
Ukhrul	8,960	2,924	2,291	1,816	932	997
Chandel	6,768	2,520	1,701	1,230	684	633

Source: Report and Tables on Age, Series-1, Census of India, 2001

* Excluding Mao-Maram, Paomata and Purul sub-divisions of Senapati district.

In Manipur, the proportion of aged population to total population is recorded as 6.71 per cent having below the nation's average (7.45 %) in 2001. Table 1 highlighted that the total population of 60 years and above was counted as 43,545 in 1961 and it increased to 145,470 with a growth rate of 234.07 per cent in 2001. The proportion to total population is however recorded as 5.58 per cent in 1961 and changed its proportion in the following decades as 6.09 per cent in 1971, 1981 (5.87%), 1991 (6.05%) and 2001 (6.71%). Growth of the aged population is depending upon the life expectancy and migration pattern. Nowaday a well health care facility is available so that the nation's life expectancy has increased and it is estimated to be 60.4 years for males and 61.8 years for females as of 1995 (M.K. Premi, 2003). Either in-migration or out-migration has also a great

Table 3
Manipur—Marital Status among the Aged Population (60+), 2001

State/District	Total	Marital Status							
		Never Married		Currently Married		Widowed		Divorced/Separated	
		% of the total population	Proportion to the total state/district population	% of the total population	Proportion to the total state/district population	% of the total population	Proportion to the total/state district population	% of the total population	Proportion to the total state/district population
1	2	3	4	5	6	7	8	9	10
Manipur*	100.00	100.00	1.86	100.00	66.98	100.00	29.62	100.00	1.54
Senapati	100.00	5.43	1.74	6.60	76.37	4.01	20.52	5.15	1.37
Tamenglong	100.00	9.78	4.17	5.09	77.98	2.23	15.12	7.80	2.73
Churachandpur	100.00	13.10	2.53	10.64	74.05	7.00	21.55	11.74	1.87
Bishnupur	100.00	7.64	1.34	10.18	64.32	11.79	32.92	9.81	1.42
Thoubal	100.00	11.63	1.31	15.88	64.36	18.49	33.14	12.77	1.19

(Contd...)

1	*2*	*3*	*4*	*5*	*6*	*7*	*8*	*9*	*10*
Imphal West	100.00	20.56	1.62	21.82	61.91	27.78	34.86	24.82	1.61
Imphal East	100.00	16.21	1.61	17.41	62.47	21.74	34.50	17.25	1.42
Ukhrul	100.00	10.30	3.11	7.23	78.63	3.54	17.04	4.88	1.22
Chandel	100.00	5.35	2.14	5.15	74.17	3.42	21.78	5.78	1.91

Source: Census of India, 2001

* Excluding Mao-Maram, Paomata and Purul sub-divisions of Senapati district.

influence to construct the present composition of state aged population.

Distribution of Aged Population

In Manipur, 145,470 aged population (60+) excluding population of Mao-Maram, Paomata and Purul sub-divisions of Senapati district is reported in 2001 of which 70.15 per cent resided in rural and 29.85 per cent in urban. The distribution of males and females are 73,233 and 72,237 respectively. Among the districts, Imphal West recorded the highest aged population with 23.61 per cent of the total population followed by Imphal East (18.67%), Thoubal (16.52%), Bishnupur (10.60 %), Churachandpur (9.63 %), Ukhrul (6.16 %), Senapati (5.79 %), Chandel (4.65%) and Tamenglong (4.37 %)(Fig. IV).

As revealed in Table 2, the total aged population is again divided into five different age groups as 60-64, 65-69, 70-74, 75-79 and 80 years and above respectively among them population of 60-64 comprised 33.09 per cent as highest followed by 65-69 (24.68 %). Among the districts, Imphal West recorded the highest aged population in all age groups while Tamenglong occupied the least in the first-four groups and the last group, i.e. 80 years and above is at Chandel. The proportion of aged population in these five age categories were highlighted in the form of age pyramid shown as state and district level in Figures I & II. In the pyramids, it is clearly shown that the lower portions of every pyramid are always made higher than the upper means 80 years and above and akin to actual pyramid form but some other developed countries like Japan it shows more or less similar population in both sexes and among the age categories.

Figure I

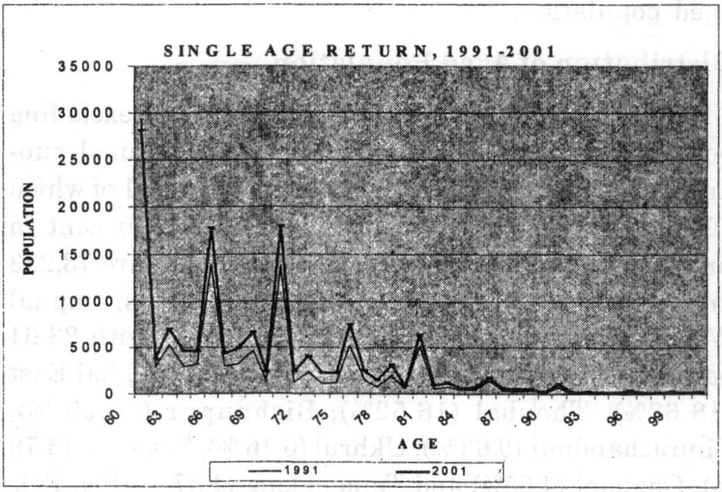

Figure II

MANIPUR: AGE PYRAMID, 2001

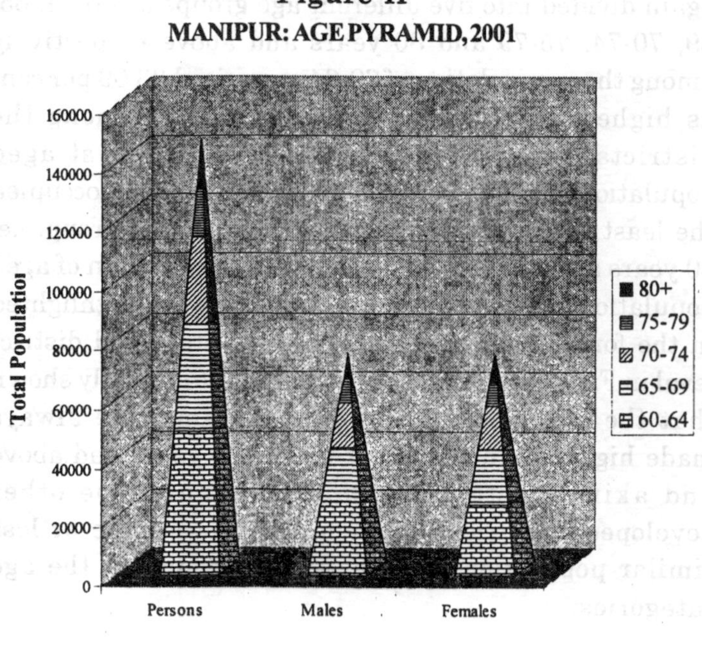

Marital Status

In simple, marital relationship between a man and a female may be known as marital status. As human societies differentiate between mating and reproduction through marriage, the institution of marriage has been found to be almost sacred and universal in the country. It is also bounded by the social and cultural milieu. So, marriage is very important for the human being, for the individual and for the society as whole and it needed be solemnized as a compulsory social norm. In Census, marital status is however, divided into four different types as never married, currently married, widowed and separated or divorced and their proportion is shown in Table 3.

Never Married: A person who has never married any time before is known as never married and it occupied 1.86 per cent of the total aged population in 2001 among them, Imphal West occupied 20.56 per cent as highest while Chandel (5.35 %) is the lowest. In another analysis that Tamenglong district calculated the highest proportion of never married persons with 4.17 per cent of the total district aged population followed by Ukhrul (3.11 %), Churachandpur (2.53 %), Chandel (2.14 %) and the remaining five districts calculated below two per cent each, among them Thoubal recorded the least (1.31 %).

Currently Married: Once life partner is chosen by means of engaging or love affairs, they should be deeming to be married. Mode of marriage pattern is different from one place to other. Marriage has become quite weak in most of the western countries and they are also allowing to marry even after having their kids but it is not solemnised in India because no one allow to have marital relationship before formal marriage by its custom and religion but remarried may be accepted if having separated/divorced or become widowed.

Currently married means, whether for the first time or another time, i.e. re-married, whose marriage is subsisting at the time of enumeration (the spouse is alive means both husband and wife are alive). It includes those persons who are recognised by the custom or society as married like 'Keina Katpa" (local name) and also for persons in stable de facto union say 'Hanjinnaba' (local name).

In Manipur, 66.98 per cent of the total aged population is recorded as currently married in 2001 and such proportion in the districts, Ukhrul recorded as highest with 78.63 per cent followed by Tamenglong (77.98 %), Senapati (76.37 %), Chandel (74.17 %) and Churachandpur (74.05 %). It indicated that all the hilly districts are above the state average, while the valley four districts are below it among which Imphal West is the least (61.91 %). As many as 21.82 per cent of the total aged currently married population is found in Imphal West as highest followed by Imphal East (17.41 %) while Tamenglong is at the bottom (5.09 %). Among the aged population, there are 148 couples recorded as 80 years and above in 2001.

Widowed: Person whose husband or wife is dead, and who is not presently re-married (at the time of enumeration/data collection) is called widowed. In 2001, the state has 29.62 per cent of the total aged population as widowed in which males are 22.22 per cent and females are 77.78 per cent respectively and it may be assumed that life expectancy rate is more in females then males or may be recorded more re-married males than females.

Imphal West district occupied the highest rate among the districts with 27.78 per cent of the total widowed population followed by Imphal East (21.74 %) while Tamenglong recorded the lowest (2.23%).

Table 4

Manipur—Migrants in Aged Population (60+) as per Birth Place, 2001

Type of Migrants	*No. of Migrants*		
	Total	*Male*	*Female*
1	*2*	*3*	*4*
In-migrant Outsider Indians enumerated in Manipur*	1,869	954	885
In-migrant Foreigners enumerated in Manipur*	689	379	310
Sub-Total:	**2,558**	**1,363**	**1,195**
Out-migrant Manipuris enumerated in other states/ Union territories	2,837	1,336	1,501

Sources: Table D-4 & D-6, Census of India, 2001
* Excluding Mao-Maram, Paomata and Purul sub-divisions of Senapati district.

Divorced or Separated: A person who is divorced either by decree of a law court or by an accepted social or religious custom but has not re-married or has been separated from wife or husband and is living apart with no apparent intention of living together again is known as divorced or separated. Few people in this category are enumerated in 2001 with only 1.54 per cent of the total aged population. The sharing of male and female divorced or separated are recorded as 34.54 per cent and 65.46 per cent.

The highest percentage of divorced or separated person is recorded in Imphal West with 24.82 per cent of the total population of this group followed by Imphal East (17.25 %) while Ukhrul is the lowest (4.88 %). Proportion of divorced or separated population to total district-aged population is however found at Tamenglong (2.73 %) as highest but the remaining 8 districts are below two per cent each.

Migration among the Aged Population

Migration is a geographic mobility that involves change of usual residence between defined political or statistical areas, or between residence areas of different types. It has been classified on the basis of physical distance, duration and period of stay, cultural and political differences, between the two places, and individual family and group migration (Joshi, S.C., 1994). As stated by Sharat Chandra (1991), migration is the transfer of people from one territorial unit to another and in the process of movement; there is redistribution of population of any territory. According to Census 2001, migration is termed as a move from one defined area (having its own jurisdiction) to another that was made during a given migration interval and that involved a change of residence also. Generally, there are two types of migrated people found in the state. They are – 1) *Immigrants* (in-migrants) – who are migrated to the state from outside and 2) *Emigrants* (out-migrants) – who are migrated from the state to elsewhere.

When a person is enumerated in census as a different place other than her/his place of birth, she/he is considered a migrant. To capture such movements of population, census collects information on migration by last residence and duration of residence as well. Migration arises out of various social, economic or political reasons. Migration may be due to marriage, which is the most common among the females or works as generally among the males.

The actual number of migrants are however collected by the Census in two ways – as per place of birth and as per place of last residence. As per place of birth, 20,677 migrants are migrated into the state in which 12.37 per cent (2,558 persons) are aged population in 2001(Table IV). In Manipur, 1,869 aged populations are migrated from the different parts of India mainland but 2,837 aged Manipuris were out-migrated from the state to other states/union territories of India in 2001. It is also recorded that 689 aged foreigners who are born abroad are also migrated in Manipur in 2001.

Table 5

Manipur-Work Participation Rate in Aged Population, 2001

Category	*Work Participation Rate (in %)*		*% of Workers to total Population*	
	Manipur	*Aged Population*	*Manipur*	*Aged Population*
1	*2*	*3*	*4*	*5*
Total Workers	43.62	56.06	100.00	100.00
Main Workers	69.80	73.69	30.43	41.31
Marginal Workers	30.20	26.31	13.19	14.75
Non-Workers		56.38	43.94	

Source: *Table B-1, Census of India, 2001*

Note: All the figures are calculated excluding Mao-Maram, Paomata and Purul sub-divisions of Senapati district.

Workers among the Aged Population

Every person has to do ones own works irrespective of age and sex whether it may be household domestic works or economic productive works. In Census, work may be defined as participation in any economically productive activity with or without compensation, wages or profit. Such participation may be physical and /or mental in nature. Work involves not only actual work but includes effective supervision and direction of work. It even includes part time help or unpaid work on farm, family enterprise or any other economic activity but does not include household chores by members of the same household. A person is categorized as worker when she/ he has participated in any economically productive activity at any time during one year preceding the date of enumeration i.e. 9-28th Febraury, 2001.

As revealed in Table 5, in Manipur, such work participation rate among the aged population is reported as 56.06 per cent against the state average 43.62 per cent of which males are 69.24 per cent and females (42.70%) in 2001. Again among the workers, it may be divided into two types as per their duration of actual work period. Firstly, it called "Main Workers" means those persons who has worked for six months or more during the last one year mentioned above and it recorded 73.69 per cent that more than thirteen per cent from the state average (69.80%) in 2001. The second one is known as "Marginal Workers". A person who has worked for less than six months (including even for a single day) is termed a Marginal Workers and it occupied 26.31 per cent that below the state average (30.20%). The Non-Workers participation rate among the aged population is 43.94 per cent that less than the state average, 56.38 per cent.

Table 6
Manipur-Percentage Distribution of General, Scheduled Caste and Scheduled Tribe Aged Population (60+) to total Population, 2001

State/District	Percentage of Aged Population to total Population of each category				Proportion of Aged Population to total Population		
	General	Scheduled Castes	Scheduled Tribes	Total	General	Scheduled Castes	Scheduled Tribes
1	*2*	*3*	*4*	*5*	*6*	*7*	*8*
Manipur	100.00	100.00	100.00	100.00	66.25	3.00	30.75
Senapati	1.60	0.11	15.36	100.00	18.34	0.06	81.60
Tamenglong	0.15	0.02	13.89	100.00	2.34	0.02	97.64
Churachandpur	0.63	0.07	29.93	100.00	4.36	0.02	95.62
Bishnupur	15.45	2.87	0.92	100.00	96.52	0.81	2.67
Thoubal	21.77	64.21	0.56	100.00	87.31	11.64	1.05
Imphal West	33.76	17.53	2.34	100.00	94.74	2.22	3.04
Imphal East	26.12	14.98	2.97	100.00	92.70	2.41	4.89
Ukhrul	0.08	-	19.86	100.00	0.86	-	99.14
Chandel	0.44	0.21	14.17	100.00	6.21	0.13	93.66

Source: *Report and Tables on Age, Series-1, Census of India, 2001*

** Excluding Mao-Maram, Paomata and Purul sub-divisions of Senapati district.*

Distribution of General, Scheduled Castes and Scheduled Tribes among the Aged Population

The total aged population of the state can be categorized into 3 groups as general, scheduled castes and scheduled tribes. In 1994, the Government of Manipur has listed four castes/communities to be included in Other Backward Classes (OBCs) as i) Meitei/ Meetei (including Meitei Brahmin, Meitei/Meetei Sanamahi, Meitei Rajkumar and non-scheduled caste Lois); ii) Meitei Pangal; iii) Telis who have been domiciled in Manipur for 10 years and their descendents; and iv) Badi (Nepali), Damai (Nepali), Gairey (Nepali), Satki (Nepali) and Kami (Nepali) who have been living in Manipur as members of the domiciled community since 09.07.1947 and their descendents (Meetei, M.M.,2007). These OBC's castes/communities are however; to be included in general category as there is no any available data on OBC in the state so far. The proportion of general, scheduled castes and scheduled tribes among the aged population are recorded as 66.25 per cent, 3.00 per cent and 30.75 per cent respectively. Predominantly four valley districts, viz. Bishnupur, Thoubal, Imphal West and Imphal East comprises general and scheduled caste population while the scheduled tribes are inhabited in the hilly five districts of Senapati, Tamenglong, Churachandpur, Ukhrul and Chandel (Table 6).

General population here includes Meiteis excluding Lois and Yaithibi of scheduled castes, Meitei Pangals and in-migrant population such as non scheduled castes Assames, Bengalis and Biharis; Marwaris; Punjabis; other Hindi speakers; south-Indians; Nepalis; and

Muslim population migrated from Pakistan and Bangladesh, etc. Among the districts, Imphal West occupied the highest percentage of general population with 33.76 per cent of the total aged population while Ukhrul (0.08%) is the lowest.

Table 7

Manipur—Literacy Rate among the Aged Population, 2001

Category/Level of Education	*Literacy Rate (in %)*
1	*2*
Total	33.70
Male	55.38
Female	11.73
a. Literate without educational level	**10.75**
b. Literate with educational level	**89.25**
1) Below Primary	20.11
2) Primary	20.40
3) Middle	21.05
4) Matric/Secondary	13.90
5) Hr.Sec./Intermediate/P.U./Sr. Secondary	3.85
6) Non-Technical Diploma or Certificate not equal to Degree	0.03
7) Technical Diploma or Certificate not equal to Degree	0.24
8) Graduate and Above	9.65
9) Unclassified	0.02

Source: Census of India, 2001

Note: Literacy rate shown excluding 3 sub-divisions of Senapati district.

Seven scheduled caste communities are recognized for the state; among them Lois and Yaithibi are the indigenous population while the remaining castes viz. Namasudra, Patni, Dhobi/Dhopi, Sutradhar and Muchi/Ravidas are originally migrated from the the states of Assam, Bengal, Bihar and Uttar Pradesh. It is stated that the Lois is the major castes, occupied 86.06 per cent of the total scheduled caste population, as thickly populated by the Lois of Kakching and Yaithibi of Thoubal, the largest scheduled caste population is recorded at Thoubal district with 64.21 per cent but there is no single scheduled caste population at Ukhrul district in 2001. Some of the noted Lois inhabited settlements are Sekmai Bazar Nagar Panchayat, Sekmai Part, Khurkhul, Kanto, Phayeng, Koutruk, Leimram Khunou (Tairenpokpi), Leimram, Andro Nagar Panchayat, Kakching Municipal Council, Kwatha and Churachandpur while Yaithibi caste; Kamu Yaithibi, Thoubal Khunou and some part of Thoubal Municipal Council were the important inhabiting areas. The scheduled caste population from outside the state are particularly settled at Jiribam sub-division of Imphal East district and some of them also resided in the various towns/market centres and headquarters. Some of them also settled at Serou village of Thoubal district.

The Government of India has listed 33 scheduled tribes in the state, namely – Aimol, Anal, Angami, Chiru, Chothe, Gangte, Hmar, Kabui, Kacha Naga, Koirao, Koireng, Kom, Lamgang, Mao, Maram, any Mizo (Lushai) tribes, Monsang, Moyon, Paite, Purum, Ralte, Sema, Simte, Suhate, Tangkhul, Thadou, Vaiphei, Zou, Paomai Naga, Kharam, Tarao and any Kuki tribes, among them, Thadou and Tangkhul are the leading tribes. The last four tribes are recognized in 2002 so that their population could not be ascertained till 2001 Census but Paomai Naga and any Kuki tribes' population may be separated from the Mao and Thadou tribes. Among the districts, Churachandpur recorded the largest scheduled tribes with 29.93 per cent and followed by Ukhrul (19.86%).

Literacy among the Aged Population

In Census, it is very simple that a person is said to be a literate when she/he can read and write in any language with understanding so that literacy rate to be calculated among the population having 7 years and above because 0-6 years of age group is counted as illiterate as they cannot know any language understandingly even though they can read and write. As noted in Table 7, the literacy rate among the aged population is 33.70 per cent against the state average 70.50 per cent in 2001. The males (55.38%) and females (11.73%) literacy rates are quit differences among the elderly peoples.

Among the literates, it can be divided into two classifications, viz. literate without educational level and it occupied only 10.75 per cent of the total aged population and literate with educational level (89.25%). Further, it can be sub-divided into 9 categories in educational level as - Below Primary, Primary, Middle, Matric/Secondary, Higher Secondary/Intermediate/Pre University/Senior Secondary, Non-Technical Diploma or Certificate not equal to Degree, Technical Diploma or Certificate not equal to Degree, Graduate and above and Unclassified. Among them, Middle class category occupied the highest with 23.59 per cent of the total literates of aged population with educational level while unclassified (0.02%) is the lowest (Table 7).

Table 8
North-Eastern India-Aged Population (60+), 2001

Country/State	Total Population	Aged Population		
		Total	Male	Female
1	*2*	*3*	*4*	*5*
India	1,028,610,328*	76,622,321(7.45%)	37,768,327(7.10%)	38,853,994(7.83%)
Total North East	38,857,769	2,262,413(5.82%)	1,158,834(5.78%)	1,103,579(5.87%)
Assam	26,655,528	1,560,366(5.85)	800,585(5.81%)	759,781(5.90%)
Meghalaya	2,318,822	105,726(4.56%)	54,016(4.59%)	51,710(4.53%)
Arunachal Pradesh	1,097,968	49,916(4.55%)	26,417(4.56%)	23,499(4.54%)
Nagaland	1,990,036	90,323(4.54%)	50,736(4.85%)	39,587(4.20%)
Manipur *	2,166,788	145,470(6.71%)	73,233(6.68%)	72,237(6.74%)
Mizoram	888,573	49,023(5.52%)	24,800(5.40%)	24,223(5.64%)
Tripura	3,199,203	232,549(7.27%)	112,656(6.86%)	119,893(7.70%)
Sikkim	540,851	29,040(5.37%)	16,391(5.68%)	12,649(5.01%)

Source: Report and Tables on Age, Series-1, Census of India, 2001
* Excluding 3 sub-divisions of Senapati district.
Figures in brackets shown percentage to total population (total/male/female).

Aged Population among the North-Eastern States

In 2001, India has a total population of 1,028,610,328 persons in which 7.45 per cent (76,622,321) is belonged to 60 years and above (aged) population. The proportion of male and female aged population to the total male and female population of the nation are recorded as 7.10 per cent and 7.83 per cent respectively. The North-Eastern India comprises 8 states, namely – Assam, Meghalaya, Arunachal Pradesh, Nagaland, Manipur, Mizoram, Tripura and Sikkim. These eight states together occupied 3.78 per cent of the total nation's population though its share in aged population is 2.95 per cent. Assam state alone constituted 68.97 per cent of the total north-eastern's aged population and it is followed by Tripura (10.28 %), Manipur (6.43 %), Meghalaya (4.67 %), Nagaland (3.99%), Arunachal Pradesh (2.21 %), Mizoram (2.17 %) and Sikkim (1.28 %) respectively (Table 8).

Table 8 also revealed that Tripura state recorded the highest proportion of aged population to total state population with 7.27 per cent in 2001 followed by Manipur (6.71 %), Assam (5.85 %), Mizoram (5.52 %), Sikkim (5.37 %), Meghalaya (4.56 %), Arunachal Pradesh (4.55 %) and Nagaland (4.54 %).

Conclusion

Nowadays, both Government of India and State Government have to give many life supportive facilities to the old aged persons either as money or kinds from time to time. Some of the NGOs have tried to establish many Old Aged Home in the state recently for those who are not having any relatives for the aged peoples. A comprehensive "National Population Policy (NPP)" was evolved and was presented to the Parliament by the then Health Minister on 16 April 1976. The Government of India wanted to introduce a National Population Policy first in 1997 and then in 1999. However, after several discussions with politicians, and a section of experts from academics, public health professionals, demographers, social scientists, and women's representatives, the Government of India presented its new National Population Policy 2000 in Parliament in February 2000. Some of the states like Andhra Pradesh, Haryana, Madhya Pradesh, Orissa, Rajasthan, Uttar Pradesh, Maharashtra and Gujarat also framed and formulated their own state Population Policies. In the latest NPP 2000, it has about "12 Strategic Themes", in which theme XI earmarked for the Aged Population mentioned as "Providing for the Older Population". In this regard we may quote the following excerpts:

> ...Improved life expectancy is leading to an increase in the absolute number and proportion of persons aged 60 years and above, and is anticipated to nearly double during 1996-2016, from 62.3 million to 112.9 million. When viewed in the context of significant weakening of the traditional support systems, the elderly are increasingly vulnerable, needing protection and care. Promoting old age health care and support will, over time, also serve to reduce the incentive to have large families.

The Ministry of Social Justice and Empowerment has adopted in January 1999 a National Policy on Older Persons. It has become important to build in geriatric health care; encouraging NGOs to design and implement formal and informal schemes that make the elderly economically self-reliant; providing for and routinising screening for cancer, osteoporosis, and cardiovascular conditions in PHCs, CHCs and urban health care centers at primary, secondary and tertiary levels; and exploring tax incentives to encourage grown-up children to look after their aged parents....(M.K. Premi, 2003).

Under this policy or provision, now it can be asked that how far the nation as well as the state have fulfilled or practiced the scheme to benefit to the needy Aged Peoples. Anyway, such a government policy is highly welcome and approaching to the concerned for fulfilling the same. Now a days harassing elderly peoples, mentally or physically, by their life supportive persons say son/ daughter or any relatives is faster increasing especially in National Capital and it needs to be minimized or to be rooted out forever. To control such barbarian behaviours, co-operation for all is required

Most of the nation's Older Persons spend their life through religions practices, recreation, etc. Ther is very little or no any recreation centres, parks or old aged home in the state. A few of them have enjoyed themselves by sitting together at the Mapan Kangjeibung or inside the Tikendrajit Park (Sahid Minar/Feidabung). Worshipping of Govindajee at Palace, worshipping of Lainingthou Sanamahi at Haying Khongban or any other God/Goddesses of Umanglai also have a room to spent their time for the some of the inhabitants resided in the valley. and the hil peoples, gathering in the Church provides a chance to exchange their views, etc. Nothing has been made so far by the Government of Manipur in these regards for the elderly peoples.

REFERENCES

Census of India, Directorate of Census Operations, Manipur: Various Publications like Report of Aged Table, Migration (1961-2001) & Religions (1991-2001).

Joshi, S.C., 1994: *Migration to a Metropolis*, RBSA Publishers, Jaipur, pp. 3-7.

M.K. Premi, 2003: *Social Demography: A Systematic Exposition*, Jawahar Publishers & Distributors, New Delhi, pp.13-290.

Meetei, M.M., 2007: "OBC in Manipur", *Sangai Daily Newspaper* April 1-3,2007.

Sharat Chandra, 1991: *Population Pattern and Social Change in India*, Hugh Publications, Allahabad.

2

SOCIAL AND ECONOMIC STATUS OF ELDERS: ISSUES AND CHALLENGES

H. Dwijasekhar Sharma

1. Death of Patriarch's Jumbo Role!

Parenting[1] is never done for profit; but surely for propagation and survival through surrogates. It was so for Chenghiz Khan; as it is now. Crudely put, parenting is the carrier system (or, conveyor-belt) between two generations. But genetically speaking, it is more indispensable like 'chicken' between one 'egg' and another in the inconclusive: "Which-came-first? Chicken-or-egg" argument. Once parenting is done, the ageing father slides low profile, while the son replicates—out to become a father himself – and descends into the world of busy bees, while the patriarch himself overarchs all three or more generations living together in 'a joint family'.

In the traditional joint family the patriarch used to give, among others, a sheen to homogenize the extended families with; bond the emotional façade of the family as a base unit of society; *and*, among others, act as a shock absorber, even when some elders were at variance with the younger generation. But he is since replaced by a system of nuclear families of binary opposites in urban settings, exposing urban nuclear families to double trouble by: *first* depriving the society of its emotional togetherness (sustenance) and stability, ultimately leading to social sclerosis (depraved morality, violence, world of money-driven society and theatre of cruelty); and *second*, throwing to the wind elders' very *raison d'etre* and socio-cultural primacy. The latter is the point of deflection for elder's current woes, deprivation, sufferings, leading to socioeconomic issues and challenges.

While considering elders' lot *vis-à-vis* sons' support etc, an analyst hardly expects to find excitement as in a thriving business leader's bargain-huntings for mergers and acquisitions. Here he condescends to family circumstances, employment and health which matter more to the elder's sense of well-being than profit or income. No doubt, richer parents with unearned (or, rental) incomes are 'happier' than the poor, as the theory goes. But beyond a threshold, the connection weakens, and more cash would not buy happiness. The broadside dictum is; once people climb out of poverty through higher income level, happiness is bound to plateau. Then even the gap between popular and elite perceptions narrow down till they converge. So argued, 'happiness' is really a proxy for something else like health. Of course, many theorists find further links between happiness, income and optimism. That said, income-bereft elders with no mundane reason to be hopeful have scarce reason to be happy about, particularly if their offspring's are themselves not well off.

2. Issues and Challenges

The "theory of mind" has much to do with ability not only to hypothesize what the elder is thinking, but to hypothesize what he is thinking about what the youth is thinking now, against then. These thought patterns are the software of behaviours and actions. The maze of introspections and thoughts would rhyme and synchronize among equals; but among unequals – say, between an instant-reacting youth and another long-reacting elder – the chain-network gets bogged down, unless the former stoops and waits for the latter's reaction. It is here that an elder is perceived as mentally slow, if not infirm. Even if he is of the non-worrying kind—not shying about if other people perceive him as aged—he preempts to stay away from life's humdrum, heavy traffic, chaotic lifestyle, rich diet etc. He would thus preempt company of likes. That is how a contagion is virtually built up in society. Following Plato's anecdote on man's cradle-to-grave journey particularly the last phase repeating the first: 'three-legged' or 'four-legged'—the youth so differentially look upon the elders' world as another, but certainly not of their kind.

Some pragmatic issues conceived herein are those arising out of inter-generational mismatch, transgressing on human and welfare dimensions; often emotion-packed with tears on sensitive, reminiscent elder's cheeks. Parental expectations or childhood memories may be behind all those emotions, complicated by former's indifferent health. It's all a matter of gaps in perceptions and perspectives: role reversal between father and son; the former now at the receiving, and the latter at giving, end; the latter putting up his 'best' effort to help, parent yet feeling 'sore' at having to ask for specific help. Being subterranean, son's help and elder's agony are kept to themselves. Nevertheless, some hypothetical worst scenario "test cases" can be taken up for two broad categories of rich and poor parents, for diversity of "logic of choice":

a) Whether and how rich and self-sustaining parents can remain buoyant while, say, their businessmen sons unfortunately slide downhill in the latter's lean spell?

b) Whether these rich and self-sustaining parents need 'decouple' themselves (*a la* China from the sliding US economy) from their sons, in case sons' business sinks into a debt trap?

c) Can miseries of poor parents, wholly-dependent on sons, be somehow averted to save the unchaperoned parents' headlong 'freefall' onto extreme penury?

d) How can most destitute, infirm parents in the unorganized sector – bereft of both own-account benefit from State and also offspring's care – be extended sustainable welfare?

e) Given parent-offspring sensitivities, how can elder be made to feel that his son is not "adding insult to injury" whenever son's promises are not complied with for compelling reasons?

f) Granted the inevitability of the 'generation gap,' how can son and father be brought onto the proverbial 'grey matters' and kept further converged without threat to, or contagion on, others and society?

Parenting, in retrospect, proved demanding; yet he gave his children more choices than he himself had. In the process he deprived himself of a possible savings to cushion his last few days in life. Besides transcending inter-generational gaps it also fuels socio-economic changes – greater demand for food, housing etc. How could he imagine to be, if ever, cast away by own children? On hindsight, he would be better off without begetting a son – but in the end it is 'argument for the sake of argument'. So the analyst has to squarely face the parent-youth matrix. Did he really wish that his sons will fix his problems in his adversity? Yes! He has a right to expect even a sporting chance that he might be looked after, unless, it so turns out that his son becomes otherwise constrained or incapable of. For that matter, the son might even predecease him. It's all those 'known unknowns'! The answer can also be: No! Because he need not look an apologist 'begging for abuse' (needy support) much less an advocate for the abused – if at all a parent condescends to beg from own son.

Hence another hypothesis, overarching all others, is in order: "Whether the surest way to buy happiness by the worthy and willing son is to give his needy father 'some of his time and money', not by way of return, but more in philanthrophy?" It doesn't matter, if the elder is getting his son's bit or time by 'default'. Mind you, only youth are given to 'irrational expectations'; while at that age, no parent expects anything beyond the direst straits. Under extreme uncertainties of poor health and perceived proximity to death, his mindset is already in a state of flux. And if the sons could provide even a fraction of their rational expectations – including personal care and attention – that should suffice and need be looked as the much-cherished 'golden handshake'.

3. "Could be Dead by Evening!"

Turning to ageing, what is its 'long and short'; or better still, what causes 'ageing'? The underlying principle (disposable soma theory) lies in the roles of structures, called *telomeres* that cap the ends of chromosomes. Every time a cell divides, its telomeres get shorter. And when they shrink beyond a certain point, that cell can no longer divide. Then even healthy tissue cannot renew itself. Hence the longer the telomere last, the longer one can expect to live. It is still unknown: why some people have longer telomeres than others, with exceptions as in case of Amish community.[2]

Gregor Mendel's basic rules of genetic inheritance remain established since 1860s: that humans and most organisms inherit two sets of genes unchanged, one from each parent. In modern terms it means one's genetic inheritance comes from the DNA that forms these genes. As of now, Mendel's law is broken, and exceptions discovered. In precise terms, other genetic information comes from places other than inherited DNA, as found true in case of twins showing different gene functions. Molecular geneticists are compiling a growing list of para-mutation. But should scientific findings and advancements least concern the feeble, famished, and often quite unconcerned progenitors?

By far, much greater perplexity of an elderly person is due to unpredictability of life – his own and that of others. As Proust once said, the greatest whimsicality is that: "[Y]ou never can be sure, you could be dead by evening." The analogous local saying is "*Ngasi sini pao-jende*! *Hayeng sini pao-takte!*" [You aren't informed: should you die today; or tomorrow!] The disconcerting part is that "Death is known, but not when you die!" On reckoning, a tripod of: treatment, respect and sympathy becomes the very pivot for specific welfare schemes to warrant elders' equipoise. Since all the three are now missing elders have none to turn to. At 70, he is lucky to be active and dementia-free, but sooner than later he may become dependent on others, if not for maintenance and nursing, but for psychological and moral support in an increasingly individualistic and violence-torn society.

4. Disenhancing Elders' Incentives

Basically, the break-up of joint family means loss of elder's social status; and advent of nuclear families implies socio-economically "empowering" his son – in the jargon of sociology, policy sciences. Far worse, disenhancing incentives of the ablebodied elder, still in his early 60s by overnight rendering him into a 'weak' social position, impairs his cognitive function.

Conversely, empowering the son sharpens his mental faculty. A lack of socio-economic power on the part of the elder almost overnight reduces his ability to keep track of information or make plans to achieve one's goals. Logically enough, if the father and son part their ways routinely, for instance, through a family arrangement, there may not be any adverse effect on the elder's psyche. Or else, the parting may itself prove to be beginning of the end of the elder.

More worryingly, there is an additional syndrome of "mis-overestimated ageing" among elders as perceived by the elder himself, such that a 60-year old deem himself "older than his actual age", by over-reacting to youth's slanting, flirtive looks, gestures, cross-references and bylines suggesting the "elder's sunset". This can be explained by a male psychology theory: people tend to think that rivals are better looking than they really are. But its corollary in case of non-rivals (empowered youth and disabled parents) would read off as: non-rivals are worse-looking than they really are. If outcomes in few cases may prove wrong, even that can come under the rescue of the error-management theory: the idea that when people make 'errors of judgment,' they tend to commit the error that is least costly. From evolutionary stance, trying and being rejected comes at a little cost, viz. hurt feelings. Not trying at all may mean loss of an opportunity to spread DNA, among others.

Sure, his societal 'status' partakes more ceremonial and cognitive nature – akin to perceptions like happiness, security – rather than activity-determining or -determined. The latter embodies a role-based (or thick) definition with accrued benefits writ large, against the former (thin) specific use, if at all, without any alternative opportunity. For instance, even in his 70s, he can in-source some responsibilities and supervise grandsons at play or study, although physically-mentally weak (passive); yet for any other gainful purpose (like marketing) he is useless. Earlier during his 'active' status characterized by 'resourcefulness' there used to be a positive correlation between activity and status. But once grown weak, problems multiply. The litmus test of a 65+ elder even in the US, being still active or not, depends very much on his health status rather than anything else.

Effects on people's cognitive faculty was studied by Dr. Pamela Smith of Netherlands and her findings reported in *Psychological Science*: stating that "low-power participants" in subordinate positions made 2-5% more errors than their "high-power counterparts" in superior positions. She argues that these results were not caused by low-power volunteers being less motivated, as they had the same financial motivation as the high-powered. She suspects that those lacking in power suffered adverse cognitive effects from that very lack, and had difficulty maintaining their focus on the task. It is all on the mind. People have been taking cognitive-enhancing drugs, just like sportpersons take performance-enhancing drugs. They work on the neural processes that underlie such mental activities as attention, perception, learning, memory, language, planning and decision-making, usually by altering the balance of the chemical neurotransmitters involved in these processes. Thus if an elder person is, as it were, pushed at the bottom of the heap, his retarded mental process may get more blunted and keep him there, lying in wait for onset of mental degradation. Interestingly, these very cognition-enhancing drugs are being regularly used to treat the effects of Alzheimer's disease, attention-deficit disorder, strokes, and the dementias associated with Parkinson's disease and schizophrenia—in the absence of any curative medicines.

5. Manipur's bulging 60+ population

In Manipur as elsewhere an elder is respected as long as he is on an activity schedule. Hence, as long as active, the most elderly in his 70s won't suffer mental agony as he is still looked up as the pride of all his kith and kin, though very much as envy of other elders. But once shrunk in oblivion, he sinks in the estimation of both kin and equals: as lacking "basic motor skills and the ability to hear, drive, stand up, straight, walk, think clearly, or provide basic financial support for him/her self." Besides being closer to infirmity, he is pushed, as it were, by his own people towards that oblivion. He might have a cognizable 'right' more on the basis of experience to participate in group-discussions, public functions; but under such hostile environment he starts selfdoubting as only half-capacitated *(or half-incapacitated?)*. Unless remedied, the benumbing psychosis accumulates as 'trauma'. Ultimately it takes away the residual 'will to live' from each and every elder in contagion.

The question of elders being 'maltreated' by society in general and offsprings in particular need be considered realistically rather than emotionally. If he still has anything to depend on like pension, as many others in the organized service, he will not feel so 'worse off'. On the one hand, without any regular income how can financial wizards create 'a future income' for him to retire peacefully? On the other, retirement is not an option for a person like him earning Rs 3,000 or so. In fact for all those like him in the unorganized sector, continued survival itself has become so very difficult, if not impossible, without help from the government and society at large. Belatedly, the government passed the Maintenance of the Welfare of Parents and other Senior Citizens Bill. But in 2004 old age pension @ Rs 100 per mensem per head was extended only to the "economically weaker section of 7,153 persons in the hill and 19,754 in valley districts": or a total of 26,907 persons at 19 per cent of Manipur's total "60+ population" of 145,470 persons (*Table 3: Col 8*) under the Manipur Old Age Pension Rules. Impactwise, it proved apparently peripheral, not at all problem-solving.

If old age is a curse in this part of the world, rural (unorganized) sector's elderly population become definitely double jinxed. And think of the large (over 80 per cent) middle-aged (below 45 years) base having irregular-income as agricultural labourers and other contract workers for just three months a year. It calls for some "financial product" of a pension scheme along Rajasthan government's innovative proxy scheme to cover 20 occupations of 5 lakh low-income workers by using technology and ground level partnership with workers Association. The Rajasthan government contributes upto Rs 1,000 per annum to motivate workers to save for their own retirement and also to ensure that the pension at the time of retirement will be above the poverty level, provided that the worker can save at least Rs 2.75 a day, and in addition, co-contribute a sum equal to that of government. Similar scheme has been launched, among others, by Madhya Pradesh,

Some glaring statistics about Manipur's age-group composition are now in order. Expectedly, demography is fast changing with higher human longevity due to advent of science, technology and medical knowledge, impacting by way of reduced rates of birth and death; since acclaimed as greater healthcare in a welfare state. Thus Manipur's "60+ population" has taken 9 decades (1911-2001) to rise from 4.2 to 6.9 per cent while "0-14 demography" declined from 43.5 to 32.6 per cent. In contrast the able-bodied "15-59 group" expanded from 52.3 to 60.5 per cent (*Appendix Table 1*) reflecting greater human potential for economic growth. A continuous rise in Manipur's '60+ composition' from 5.8 per cent to 6.1, 6.9 per cent (*Appendix Table Nos.1*) respectively over 1961, 1991, 2001 shows an interesting parallelity to corresponding national data of 5.63, 6.58 and 7.08 per cent. Thus the projected (2021) "60+ demography" of Manipur may well approach 9.87 per cent, estimated for the nation (*Yadav: 2004*). This works out at one elder for every nine non-elders, *or one for every two households of 5 inmates each* – involving greater dependency on youth, as well as liability for the State: old age homes, cradle-to-grave medical care, innovative pension benefits and yet other elder-specific reliefs.

Of course, the comparable global composition estimate of 5.3 per cent (1980) did prove lower than

Manipur's 6.0 per cent (1981). Yet the former has since risen much faster to 7.7 per cent by 2000 (more than Manipur's corresponding 6.9 per cent). Thus Manipur's estimated (2025) "60+ composition" may be higher but perhaps well below 13.3 percent, estimated for global population. Over 1991-2001 the "60-69 population" exhibits the lowest 21 per cent growth *(Table 2 Col. 4)*, against the two next higher "70-79" and "80-and-above" age groups respectively exhibiting 50 and 45 per cent growth. Recalling that the current "60-69 agegroup" were born in the wake of W.War II ravaging Manipur, the staggered growth seems but natural. In fact, the growth of those subsequently born viz. those in "70-79" and "80-and above" exhibited due growth.

Census (2001) also exhibits another significant change in terms of greater female longevity and associated greater female-to-male ratio in the "60+ Imphal urban population" as below.

Imphal Urban Population by Broad Age groups: 2001

Age-group	*Persons*	*%*	*Males*	*%*	*Females*	*%*	*Col4-6)*
(1)	*(2)*	*(3)*	*(4)*	*(5)*	*(6)*	*(7)*	*(8)*
All ages	228,419	100	113,227	100.00	115,192	100.00	(-) 1,965
0-14	59,424	26	30,091	26.58	29,333	25.46	758
15-59	150,052	66	74,385	65.70	75,667	65.69	(-) 1,282
60+	18,600	8	8,541	7.54	10,059	8.73	(-) 1,518
ANS	343	-	210	0.18	133	0.12	77

Source: *Imphal Urban Parts under Imphal West and Imphal East Districts under Appendix Table 6*

ANS : Age not stated

The latest Imphal urban "60+ data" also reveal females comprising a marked 8.73 per cent of the total gender population, marginally higher than male. In absolute terms both the ablebodied "15-59" and the higher "60+ " agegroups hereinabove exhibit respectively around 2 and 15 per cent more females than males – surely not as sudden, irregular spurt, but as an embedded, long term trend. Greater female advantage could stem from only better management of lifestyle 'change', accruing from positive fundamentals.

6. Exclusive Gender Domain

Tellingly, Manipur's gender spectrum was characterized by something unique and exceptional, since time immemorial. Embattled Manipur's entire range of non-military (civil) affairs did embody female domain, because all husbands used to be battle-worn – and even when available at home for a few days – hardly disposed to farming. But how females managed to fit the role, and bear the brunt, of family management (including cultivation) on their slender frame still remains a grey area. All battle-dislocated household economies of Manipur were in effect "relocated" by housewives. Did fear psychosis of war-associated violence (including husband 'brought home dead') task her for such "second line of defence"? Her exclusivity lies: *first,* in not underestimating herself as inferior gender; *second,* perfectly fitting the robust male role – of course with help of adult sons – effortlessly, ungrudgingly and showing least signs of fatigue due to overstretched effort over time; *third* without herself becoming (or claiming) the titular head of the family (as in a matriarchal family). It was not a show of feat, much less a challenge from either society or husbands. Any female would reply back: "It was competition against words, not the people." On hindsight one may introspect if the then evolved gender empowerment was premature—for instance, should it have proved more beneficial, had they been educated and idea-embellished as of now? Or, was it a case of "willing housewives" subjugated by "indulgent husbands" – vis-à-vis the since cherished policy of "gender empowerment" to transform female dependency on male into full-fledged female participation on par with male?

Females of Manipur used to be the 'main bread-earners' themselves – the opposite of *Purdah nashin* women abstaining hard work, particularly outside home. It is because males used to fight wars in the service of royalty, hence away from home for long periods – in waging war on Assam to the west or Burma in the east – in return for which the king would allot one *pari* (=hectare) of farm land to sustain the family. Thus the housewives, more often than not, would even plough the field, lest they miss rain-fed farming and the family gets starved next year. Of course, the off-farm season would see young housewives engaged in handloom weaving etc while widows, divorcees and middle aged females would be more active as traders in the Imphal market, with marketing network (*read*, supply chain contacts, *ma-ngais*) all over hills and valley. The point is that females used to be otherwise also fully engaged in non-sedentary household chores (paddy-handpounding, kitchen gardening, fishing, trading) and would run the household with the help of offsprings, while males – in off-*lallup* duties – lead a relaxed life, oft-indulging in polygyny after royalty and nobility. Strictly speaking, Manipur had: not a male-centered society, as oft-claimed; but proactive 'means-tested' females sustaining household economies, at some notches above Henrik Ibsen's implicit role when he said: "Woman is judged by masculine law"(*A Doll's House: 1880*). Exceptionality lies in ungrudging females' self-enhanced civil role transcending over millennia-old history of patrilinear Manipur – otherwise absolutely male-centered with king Pakhangba as Supreme God, while at lower religio-cultural levels, the clan themselves used to be as more ancestor-centered, with clan ancestors worshipped as lesser Gods in specific altars and temples[3].

But then, perhaps only for being so bold, and economically overactive, females of Manipur had to die younger than males, till 2001. Appendix: Table 3 precisely shows lesser '60+' female (1991) than male population at 47: 53, against opposite trend in the world: *viz.* "fair sex outlives male". The argument-stopping theory is that males have to compete for female attention while females are not subject to that inherent gender pressure. Obviously that takes a greater toll on male. As of now, most students of "ageing" agree that one's maximum lifespan is set by how long one can reasonably expect and actually escape disease, accident, indulgences (polygamy), damaging aggression by others. It is environment, they concur, that affects longevity. Hence for the world at large, female environment, including medicare, maternity, work-life balance, urbanization, etc are generally so congenial that most die of old age, but scarcely during or after child birth. On that score feminists the world over have little complaint.

But, as per 2001 Census data, the 1991-trend has since been not only halted, but an opposite trend thrown up by '60+ male' population (2001) being slightly less at 6.68 per cent of total male, against females' 6.74 per cent of total female demography. However the "total 60+" 2001 males (*Appendix Table 3: Col 10 &12*) continue to still outnumber females in the ratio of 50.3 to 49.7 – possibly as traces that will wipe out as younger generation come of age. Although still wafer-thin, it speaks volume as a trend-setter, marking the end of a long spell of females predeceasing males in general. To prove the counterpoint, some clear trends can be discerned over 1991-2001:

i) female composition improves *vis-à-vis* male, in all age-groups and total categories, except "60-64" (*Appendix Table 3: Col 7 &13)*, implying that more females now outlive males;

(ii) female centenarians (2001) become double of male counterparts (*Appendix Table 4: Cols 4- 5*); true in both hill and valley, except Ukhrul registering more male centenarians [*Table 4: Col 6* shows the districtwise & environment-wise female-male ratios];

(iii) valley districts (Imphal urban area) exhibit higher "60+ population" in 2001, clustering well above 7 per cent of total demography (*Appendix*

Table 5: Col 9 & 11), against 6 per cent in hills districts, reflecting a changing lifestyle in turn impacting on longevity;

(iv) Female predominance over male in "60+" and "15-59" groups is also shown by Scheduled Caste (SC) population (*Appendix Table 7*), although district-level data not shown; *and.*

(v) Gender ascendancy is still not exhibited by the Scheduled Tribes (ST) population (*Appendix Table 8*) who are possibly just changing over from a leisurely-living lifestyle (non-users of time) to faster activity modules (time-users), very much affirming the hypothesis.

Granted further changes in terms of continuing urbanization, Manipur's unique pre-1991 exceptionality may soon get reversed – converging onto the global pattern. As to clearer impact of urbanization on longevity, the Manipur valley districts, particularly urban areas (*Appendix Table 4 and 6*) hint a positive correlation, although its impact on male and female separately need gender-specific analysis on the basis of empirical data.

7. Living Dead

Above all, the advent of Westernization, democracy and competition shook the very foundation of all feudal institutions, including joint families, leading to a simultaneous rise of individualism and nuclear families. Now educated and globally employable youth forsake native homes on the sly in search of greener pastures leaving behind elders rather alone, helpless, destitute, forlorn and uncared for. Globalism has eroded the primodial role of patriarchs of the family, clan, tribe very much within their own active lives. So complete is the dilapidation of all existing traditions, that the prospect of unbothered living has become dim towards the fag end of life and it is now agreed that cheerier formulations and modules need be labeled, given that they need die earlier than the youngsters. Despite real-time e-connectivity including Skype visual-voice call service between parents and sons working abroad, familial love and patron's survival are at stake in a fast-track globalized world.

Relevant herein is another query: whether the status of the family patriarch has also suffered an "authority deficit", in league with authority itself draining away from international institutions, nation-state itself, other social institutions, including family? Less authority is not always a bad thing. Some may argue, it is just a corollary for equal power among differentiated hierarchies. But it makes the society less orderly and thus less secure. Under such constraints can the patriarch pull himself and his clan up by own effort (*read* shoestrings)? But, "[a]ll that he wants is security only. He has no ambition, as such....Every parent wants to leave behind a thriving replicate....There is no light at the end of the tunnel because parental choice may not always prevail."

Themselves not well off in their peak days – and otherwise Manipur being a low work-ethic state – most retirees are left with little savings. But even if offsprings come forward to readily meet part of their maintenance in either parental homes (old age homes yet to come up in this part of the country), or otherwise, then the elders' psyche may still feel *unloved, uncared for* or *wanting that extra "soft something*" – affordable only in a happy home. That too towards their journey's end. As if each elder *is an island*, out of bounds for his own descendents. One and all, though, may not have lived upto that ever-shining ideal. For instance, on the asset side elders are less likely to accrue more social and economic inventories or accumulated savings. In fact there are greater chances that most elders, requiring relocation in old age homes, belong to poor or low middle income group in a state like Manipur where 17.3 per cent of the population remains below poverty line. In such BPL households elders deem themselves as a burden on their not-so-well-off sons. In other words, ecologically speaking, the symbiosis between father and son undergoes a change: *mutualism* (both-working-father-and-son-benefit) turns into *parasitism* (handicapped father benefits; but working son suffers). Needless to add, in the entire process, the centre of economic gravity shifts to the son.

But where the son's interest (or success) itself depends on his remaining in the family fold (succession)—as when the father is in a position to leave behind a family fortune or a successful family-owned firm – the son may preempt not to fall out with the father but to await his inheritance. Or else ambitious sons may scarcely care for "pop-and-mom" (street-corner) shops. Even otherwise, any case of father's undiminished economic gravity is merely coincidental or at best a happenstance.

8. Creative Imagination and Prediction

'Old is gold' resounds one and all, in awe and respect for old age, even if his cognitive resonance is fading. "In the long run we are all dead" Keynes said somewhat sheepishly, as elders' interest fades, and we do not perhaps care even if the facts find us out. Or else, the average *elder* (if still able-bodied) excels in having a full range of human memory, emotions and reactions that go with it. That's as long as their neurons do not relapse and fail their fleeting memories whenever the occasion demands. For instance, besides recalling through some conscious effort that Manipur's average per capita income was Rs 19,625 (*Advance estimate*) in 2006-07 at constant (1999-00) prices, against Rs 22,379 for All India [*Economic Survey: Manipur: 2007-08: Govt of Manipur: p.28*], an elder, like all others, will naturally have many other watershed memories of happiness, love, bravery, loss, cynicism and regret. He has acquired maximum experience from his lifelong work. That is the all-comprehensive broad-banding halo for elderly wisdom, technical knowhow and intuitive skill and differential approach to unsurmountable problems. Thus Japan avails the creativity, innovation and work ethics of employees till their last breath – no retrenchment from their life-long service. Japan thus makes maximum use of the human capital. Naturally with all their lifetime savings plus all the other assets they are held with awe and greatest adulation, besides mitigating geriatric problems.

What about creative imagination and prediction? Perhaps these all associate with something unexplainable on a purely structural or functional basis. Characteristically brimming in an elderly mindset is the human spirit. For as one becomes older one finds solace in seeking the inner meaning of life, the fundamental difference between the *living dead* and *dead living*. This is where religion and science will join together one of these days and tell the fundamental difference between life and death. Generally an elder gets much more *stimuli stored as memories at the conscious level*. In contrast a greenhorn may have only *responses to stimulus in the subconscious level*. Going by this theory, one does not store stimuli, one only stores responses to stimuli. From age zero and earlier, one stores responses which become one's subconscious. The task of psycho-analysis is to help bring subconscious responses into consciousness, where one can take charge of them. And so long as they remain subconscious they are in charge of one's (youth's) mind. Alas! but for these angry youth, the world would be much more serene.

Likewise, in society the longest survivor alone would outlive the largest number of problems, hence acquired wisdom from as many solved/unsolved problems – in fact the *problem of problems*. He becomes the core human capital, if at all he is able-bodied enough to share it with the less fortunate. Incidentally, this explains why youth succumbs more often to emotions while elders remain cool, placid and unprovoked by passing storms – the worst case scenarios. Its corollary being that even a known reactionary youth gets visibly normalized as he attains old age. Some people show the cellular signs of dementia without being demented. Those telling scene of Alzheimer's patients brought for admission in local hospital are surest signs for the oppressed wife to feel: "He is just alive, but already incapable to live all by himself with little nuisance value." And Alzheimer is such a disease that the longer one lives, the more likely he is to get it. The richer patients are not much of a problem, but average and Below Poverty Line (BPL) patients can best be looked after by State. As average life-expectancies rise, so will the incidence of this long-lingering disease. Also, no one really knows so far why it debilitates and kills and how to treat it.. Medical advance means that other diseases are failing to cull the population before Alzheimer destroys people's minds. Even in the US it cost its patient $ 1,74,000 between diagnosis and death.

9. Death of Expertise & Experience

Yet, elder's basic quality due to intuition is soon to end because of the fasttrack growth of technology. The halo of *intuition and flair* is threatened by *automated decision-making*: computer-enabled processes to surpass human experts in fields as diverse as rating wines, writing film dialogues and choosing titles for books. Hitherto highly-paid professional jobs as bank-loan officer is now replaced by a mere call centre operative, and paid peanuts just to parrot the words a computer prompts. For that matter doctors are challenged by computers who can diagnose diseases better, as are teachers, although their presence may still be necessary to engage their pupils.

Every time a world-class chess player loses to a computer, humans die a little. It presents a convincing and disturbing vision of a future in which everyday decision-making is increasingly automated, and the role of human judgment restricted to providing input to formulate (more like a call centre operator). That is a definite pointer to death of expertise. But till that doomsday of *end of intuition* for the elderly [or automated and perhaps least costly decision-making in all conventional disciplines], let *old be gold!*

10. Zero-sum Game (?)

Two failings stand out in the parent-son's mutual blame-game. One is that parent would hardly ever master the trick played so deftly by the son of over-dressing his own interest beyond his meager resources as if it was all due to parent's own 'parenting deficiency'. Another is that most analysts portray the "father-son game" largely in "zero-sum" terms, in which either father or son wins, but never both: as in a "win-win" situation. But then a policy scientist scans for a transformational role of society in general and geriatrics in particular; not for *a zero-sum game* between parent and son; *e.g. either* former's gain and latter's loss; *or* former's minimal welfare and latter's unavoidable sacrifice. Neither loses but both gains howsoever little in a positive-sum game, if at all father and son gel together. The lot of the elder can be made tolerable – that is if at all he commandeers enough patience and stoicism that calms down his own stress. He needs, if possible, re-balance the material and human relationship between him and the son across the generation chasm. The son also has to adjust under *mutualism symbiosis*. What matters is that supreme relationship between two *species/identities* of the same social unit – erstwhile breadwinners and current sustainers. Both father and son need gain that extra holistic pleasure of making their lives *liveable* – and, at that, the humane aspect of two self-respecting subspecies just one generation apart. After all, the self-effacing but proactive elder still wants to hear what he has professed, practiced and believed as his motto throughout his life.

Even if the parent has no pension/savings to fall back upon, besides being *computer-averse,* let him hear only what he fancies till his end! On scrutiny, the basic conflict is encapsuled as the battle (*read symbiotic parasitism*) between youth not converging onto the old. The child accuses (or inwardly blames) the elder of something without realizing how *deep his own shortcomings are*. Similarly the elder accuses the child of something but not himself at the same time. A compatibility dialectics thus lie between one generation and the next; between the blamed and the blamer; about who passes on what to whom, if at all a lesson be learnt from King Lear.

Cynicism is a luxury for those who watch inter-generational conflicts as a sport. Despair, pessimism and inaction had been at the roots of social conundrum. It has now become a proxy vote for militant absolutism on the part of elder-sceptics. *Prima facie*, the generational gap looks unbridgeable: "The young think the old are fools. But the old know the young are idiots." Yet peace between estranged parents and offsprings is not a problem. Anyone can restore it; by making both positive in approach and looking upon the other as real benefactors, not pretenders play-acting. More as friends rather than as father and son, if the grieving parent could show more gratitude while the son greater magnanimity the dividing line will get blurred. Making love beats making wars, it seems.

11. Culture of *Cluster Policy Thinking*

Most quizzically, some *greening* perspective becomes due, as the very ageing process seems *slow* for Manipur elders, whereas mainstream elders seem to become more prematurely weak, grey-haired and emaciated than Manipur counterparts here, as if the Keynisian dictum that "we are all dead in the long run" applies much more fully for them but not for Manipur. Mention 'elderly' to Manipuri elders and they go misty-eyed with a flash-back of two millennia. For most elders – often found congregating in morning/evening walk-arounds, local fora, religious gatherings or campfires – life seems unending – altogether oblivious of the boredom, stress and strain. Seemingly they adhere to: "What is this life, if there is no time to stand and stare (*read gossip and explode in laughter*)." Through king Bhagyachandra's magnanimous effort, the aged have the 18th century been provided a self-effacing platform for regular afternoon/evening pastimes of listening to serial epic stories: *Ramayana*, *Mahabharata* etc throughout the valley. And till date they seem to get lost in the conundrum of religious dialectics or historial episodes – thereby slowing down the ageing process – rather than sitting desolate and gloomy in a corner of his house or else with a distant look.

So aptly would Sogyal Rinpoche bring out the contextuality between living and death whereby death must be addressed by both youth and elders as "the balanced perspective on dying":

"The fate of the gods reminds me of the way the elderly, the sick and the dying are treated today. Our society is obsessed with youth, sex, and power and we shun old age and decay. Isn't it terrible that we discard old people when their working life is finished and they are no longer useful? Isn't it disturbing that we cast them into old people's homes, where they die lonely and abandoned?" (*The Tibetan Book of Living and Dying*: 2002).

The world is spiky. One and all without exception are subject to booms and busts; happiness and despair; *or* health and sickness. Hence while still alive and kicking, the elders, immediately in their threshold stage need apply and practice cluster thinking for productive purposes. Thus the safest and surest method to cash in on human capital (expertise, experience and innovation) is to incentivize cluster-policy thinking among both technocrat and non-technocrat elders so as to find combinations of hard and soft infrastructure problems. Danish philosopher Kier Kegaard famously wrote that *life is lived forwards, but understood backwards*. This is very true for the non-elders. But once someone becomes old, the opposite law holds: *life is lived backwards* (in flashbacks or old memories) *but understood forwards* (with a redefined meaning). Clusters are good in any field because they boost commonality in approach to social problems, seeking to reduce constraints and encourage externalities to raise productivity of competition. Cluster policy thinking is different from industrial policy thinking though many economists lump the two together. Cluster theory is neutral, rather than about picking winners. Networked elders could be a catalyst for better relations with non-elders, as well as seeking cradle-to-grave healthcare etc from government. A solid social solidarity is the quintessence of elder's innermost longing to live on and on. Such solidarity need be integrated and proactivated by both the social fabric and State apparatus.

12. Post-retirement Blues

No doubt, some ablebodied retirees with "second literacy" (IT-enabled) are fortunate enough to grab some job to supplement their meager pension, depending on their expertise and experience being still put to good use, even if not recycled. A majority preempt to retire gracefully, graciously too, with a job-well-done-satiety mindset (having played their innings to their satisfaction). But retirement can be a bane for those who did not plan their future so as to afford the kind of lifestyle that one should normally lead. Or, may be, they have been expecting more physical, financial and other help. Naturally then frustration sets in, which will make them beg undue favours from the government. Sky is the limit for one's desire to acquire more assistance or comfort. One person's adequacy may not be true for another. A peaceful life is warranted, not by material comfort alone, but more importantly by abstinence. Wantlessness, though, is the more achievable virtue as a person becomes older. For instance, the post-superannuation period is the most convenient time – and social status – when books can be attempted on beloved subjects, either taught or pursued for well over three decades, provided one has the time and patience for quiet reflection, turning a construct 180 degrees or deconstructing is for re-engineering purposes. Comparing his productivity with that of a teacher proceeding on furlough just to write a book, he need not be underwhelmed by retirement. More like these esteemed teachers who keep shuttling on post-retirement assignments from one Western university to another, almost unendingly.

With the six-digit pay-cheques, the youth may not be all that happy and contented. As Gandhiji once famously remarked: "There is enough wealth in the world for man's need, but not for man's greed." This is hardly surprising, because real income is likely to be only one element in a person's happiness, and as economic theory postulates diminishing marginal utility from increased income (consumption) we would expect rich countries to have reached what Frank Ramsey postulated as the "Bliss" level of utility. These complaints about the psychologically dysfunctional effects of capitalism confuse questions about how best to make a living (material beliefs), with those concerning, in Plato's words, how one should live (cosmological beliefs). Capitalism provides a new and highly productive way of making a living. Whilst its social ills, like the decline in family values and companionship, have less to do with capitalism than individualism. It is the demoralization of their societies rather than the instrument of their prosperity – capitalism – which is to be blamed for the social ills cited by the happiness researchers.

What can be done to immediately overcome geriatric vulnerability; and imbibe positivism, uprightness and competitive spirit among elders? "Precious little, as it is deeply embedded in the very socio-economic system, institutions, mindset and conservatism." Deconstructing the relevant issue over a time frame it can be redefined as: "When and how can desperate elders here (*read* in this part of the globe) be delivered?" Of course, it's their own doing; for most of them are still in the thick, corrosive, colonial mindset and (even the ablebodied) lack the innate will to live life full-bloodedly – in sharp contrast with the innovative, short-circuitative or '(medically) invasive treatment' mindset of their sons. Even if there is little that (s)he can do about her/his own deliverance and thus keep waiting (for Godot?), their lot will gradually improve, as and when the poor are brought above the poverty line as per policy scientists' targets and achieved objectives. So, at least, there is an obvious air of optimism, despite current geriatric problems being fundamentally linked to poverty (*read* socio-economic inequality). It looks though the geriatric culprit is neither the growing materialism nor the shallow culturalism that goes with materialism.

But obfuscating the geriatric problem here is the inherent psychosis among ablebodied sons being still unreconciled to the factum of greater longevity of their parents, even while the society fails to transform and rise to the occasion. For in open forums and without any sign of hesitancy for elders' status in society, they are still referred to, much less as "Grand old man!" but more often as, "Ye, Oldie!"? The society need thus transform its mindset from a passive-syndrome (*read* derisive mindset) to an active state, while the government itself shifts its paradigm from employer-cum-dispenser-of-welfare to a facilitator or catalytic agent to generate the adventuresome mode of self-reliance. Pending that social transformation, government need provide: (a) means-tested livelihood (self-employment avenues) and raise the superannuation age in government service: say, to 65 years (even if not lifelong, as in Japan); and (b) geriatric institutions like old age homes *and* geriatric healthcare and other specific needs of long-lived elders.

13. World's Oldest Man Passes Away!

The 'take' of the 3-digit centenarians of Manipur may well be "how to live longer?" Not just these centenarians, all others will eat their heart out. But its obvious corollary is "how to keep fit as a fiddle?" It's not a miracle; it involves much more than a mere click of the mouse to put elders on that trajectory. A whole new resonance and feeling of togetherness is highlighted by the International Conference on Satisfactory Longevity in May 2006 in Cuba. Of all places having the longest-lived human beings, like Japan, Cuba is one where it is assumed that there is even a connection between long life and Marxist dialectics (*keeping the brain ever resonant*), among others. In that conference sang not a nameless, but a towering Mercedes Matilde Nunez, aged 102, while Professor Eduardo, 104, waltzed around to the tune of *Almendra* and Amada Hernandez Fernandez, 102, announced that she should really be in the kitchen, cooking up a storm of rice, chicken and vegetables with plenty of garlic and coriander. The star of the show was Benito Martinez Abrogan, 125, who preferred to stay 240 miles east breeding fighting cocks, growing bananas and tripping the light fantastic with any young nurse he could grab at the senior citizens' centre. This possibly world's oldest man died on October 11, 2006 aged around 120.

"Martinez certainly got exercise. He was a labourer all his life, cutting sugar cane (on Castro's father's ranch) and helping build the Central Highway. Like most Cubans he had no car; he biked or walked barefoot or waited for bus with patience and stoicism that calms down stress. Asked the secret of his youthfulness, he said he had never cheated a man or said bad things of other people. And he had a good socialist motivation to survive; he wished, someday he would shake Castro's hand." *The Economist: Oct 21st 2006: London: p.89*)

Then alone he can perhaps hopefully live at least as centenarians, as Cuba has shown in terms of world's best healthcare. *A fountain of perpetual youth*, amidst El Dorado and yet other dreams of mountains of silver, did once attract Europeans and stout Africans to the New World. And their descendents – the Cuban centenarians—are now tilling the field and dancing with the energy of young men. While Eastern spirituality highlights the need for moderation in eating, Western precepts come much more specific by establishing even an inverse relationship between life and eating: *Eat less and live one-fifth longer.* Surely Cubans add at least one perquisite – tough physical exercise.

14. Eat More Greens to Fight 'Ageing'?

It looks unlikely that medical science will abolish the process of ageing. But it no longer looks impossible. True. But longevity can still be increased through, for instance, under-eating, The paradoxical desire to live longer is opposed to another evolutionary force – the disposable *soma* or body. The evolutionary logic is: you need a body to evolve, more or less like chicken for having the next genetic line – sheer illogic to have egg from egg direct. Hence Dr de Grey factorizes ageing into seven components and deals with all the seven factors so as to slow down ageing, even if not stopping. He calls his methodology "strategies for engineered negligible senescence" (SENS). The seven manageable subprocesses are: (1) cell loss; (2) apoptosis-resistance (tendency of cells to refuse to die when they are supposed to die); (3) gene mutations in the cell nucleus; (4) gene mutations in the mitochondria (the cell's power-packs); (5) accumulation of junk inside cells; (6) accumulation of junk outside cells; *and* (7) accumulation of inappropriate chemical links in the material that support cells. Significantly, the last five are oxidation-related.

Mitochondria are where sugar is broken down into and reacted with oxygen to release the energy needed to power a cell. Without oxygen, in stead of reacting with carbon from the sugar to form carbon dioxide, it would form highly reactive molecules, called free radicals. These go around oxidizing and damaging other molecules, such as DNA and proteins, which cause all sorts of troubles. Consuming vitamin C, other vitamins and other antioxidants could pep up the activity of mitochondria of elderly persons. Death cannot perhaps be defied but people can outlive the limit imposed by disposable somas through repair of the worn-out parts or damaged ones with new ones through regenerative medicines using stem cells techniques – now painstakingly being researched into, ever since innovated by one founder of scientific gerontology: Bruce Ames of California University, Berkeley. Meanwhile, the battle against ageing has continued on yet other fronts.

15. Eat 3/4th only to live 1/5th of Life Longer

Gluttons, for instance, risk various ailments. Extrapolating from this, one can choose to undereat so as to lead a healthier (non-obese) *soma* (body). If the process of body's wear and tear can only be slowed down, much relief will be brought about for instance by ingesting only 3/4ths of our normal calorie intake. Among others, elders can remain healthier if they remain on a diet of about 1,800 calories for sedentary male and 1,500 for sedentary female. In theory only the brain couldn't be plausibly replaced through stem cells because any such replacement would have to replicate the pattern of its nerve cells precisely so as to preserve an individual's memory and personality. Experimentation on threadworm, mice, etc has proved that putting an animal on a diet near, but not quite at, starvation-point prolongs life sometimes rather dramatically; although not so far done on humans. The way calorie restriction prolongs life revolves round genes for proteins called sirtuins. Surely these genes are involved in life extension in threadworms and mices. 'Eat lean and vegetarian!' is another wisdom established by observing dietetic habits and longevities of ethnic groups. By that standard the French consume fatty diet and lot of red meat, but paradoxically enough consume lot of red wine, which contains a molecule called resveratrol found in such wine. Resveratrol activates sirtuins and some similar molecules are also found to be super-stimulants.

As a result of all these exposures, if at all one can decelerate ageing, thereby converging onto the evolutionary response to starvation rather than as a weird accident? Doubtful! Although hopefully "dawn can be recycled in life's dusk," sort of, through elder's own willful deeds, lifestyle and abstinence. Chances are that mankind will never be eternal. At least, hope springs eternal, though. One can rhyme with Woody Allen: "I don't want to achieve immortality through not dying." Unless that chance factor pops up and a researcher manages to beat evolutionary history, when he can achieve both kinds of immortality.

16. Ethics & Liability of Geriatric Challenges

Yet the richest son can not still buy immortality for his loving, "doing well, but not well enough" parent. Even if he is favourably disposed, it is not on sale. Attempts, though, are being made to have a reinvigorated lease of life, being made in this fast changing society. Yes, there is a mad scramble for scientific research and there is no knowing when new values – not necessarily, good and enduring – will overtake traditional ones. "Our family" has become "my family" consisting of own consort and children only. Hence the "do-nothing, vulnerable" elder has to accommodate himself to another set of values, rather than muttering to his son: "till I die, you live with me". Further if his daughter-in-law is also working, then naturally "old age home" may prove a better – Hobson's— choice. In a way, it's better than the lot of those middle-aged parents taken along by sons working in the US, to look after their babies (baby-sitting there being costlier than paying for parent's airfare and upkeep). Sounds better than asking parents here routinely to sit or escort babies at home and schools inland! But do parents have a choice?

The dividing line between those incapacitated elders and the ablebodied lot in society is basically the 'efficiency line' which separates users from nonusers of time; or those who can work from those who can't. But the question of an 'efficiency line' is ruled out on account of his elderly status and he can't bring himself make do for any other thing than taking rest all through those 24 x 7 hours. To put a little precision into the argument, (s)he has nothing else to gainfully spend his/her time: or that his/her opportunity (second best) cost is nil. If (s)he can cook and do household chores, so much the better. Or else, even that is to be provided.

Youth need also be both positive and tolerant. It's more like de-coupling of a railway train – son's train from the father's. In the changed world, they ought to have some non-negotiable values – based on their love and affection for their parents. Then both will gain and cherish a sustained, shared value. A fundamental "rebalancing" of the relationships between nucleating families would help in managing the ongoing social change process, and yet re-define shared values between own parents and sons. Whichever explanation is correct (and both might be) senior citizens need be spared the mental trauma of being looked upon as a load/burden on the existing system. Recalling that their mobility is restricted, body joints in pain, vision and hearing impaired, it takes much longer for them to do normal things. And a young passer-by on the busy road may not appreciate the challenges faced by elder in trying to cross over, or board a bus, tram or train and is bound to become rude and impatient. To counter this behaviour, it is important to properly train the staff on how to relate to and service the senior citizens as infirm. There is more to the problem than meets the eye. "Youth can't unburden either the ethics or liability of maintaining geriatric destitutes."

But society is changing fundamentally. Youth no longer remain youth of yesterday. Old leadership models, based on what people used to be like, cannot be effective for youth of today. Offsprings of joint families used to be moulded in the dominant male structure; much different from those in nuclear families, where authority is shared between the father and mother. It appears that many employees raised in non-traditional families feel stronger ties to sibling figures than to parental-type bosses. Dad is dead as a role model. The society has transformed where youth are looking for father figures in their bosses. Youth have become independent "interactives", with readiness for change, and a quick ability to connect with others and work in a self-managed team. Many of them have grown up playing video games with people around the world, who thus feel at home in a global economy. Typically, transference is the emotional glue that binds people to a leader that makes them want to follow, even where they are unclear about where the leader is taking them.

17. Adapt and Counter-adapt!

More to caution overdependent parents, and less to foreclose sons' reciprocal love for parents, there goes a local saying: "*Turel ichel-di kadou-ngeida hang-gat-tuna chende!*" [River current never flows upstream!] In its long course from origin to ocean, could it ever? For then the natural process of rainwater-riverflow-seawater-precipitation would all get dislocated, throwing the entire climate change cycle, farming etc overboard. Yet the "impossibility" becomes an exception as when the swollen water of a tributary forces the main river's water upstream at least until the water level flows normal. Likewise, the religiosity involved in Manipur's "ancestor worship" system makes out the golden exception to the general rule: affection hardly reverse across inter-generational spectrum.

It is an arms race – a matter of adapting and counteradapting. The better the elder adapt to the nuclear family society and minimize his burden, the more host son and daughter-in-law can improve their ability to extend minimal care for the aged – like meeting the father every Sunday. Where all these are not possible, one may as well 'timepass' or show off pretensions even if not genuine love and affections, to keep the flickering flame of hope alive. Recall: a few years earlier both father and son overstretched each other's capacity to reciprocate one other's love. But since then the father has grown older, and less confident and more vulnerable. Then, neither would mind leaving own finances in disarray. Now at least the father can no longer replenish his resources, even if overstretched. Hence more than anytime earlier he has become vulnerable and he needs a helping hand. More than anything else, elders need be emotionally balanced themselves, so as not to allow their expectations to degrade below a reasonable level.

Children are on the way of becoming a mere consumer good, thereby very much threatening the human basis of the future generation. By rewriting our own operating instructions (*a la* computer software or driver) we can change our relationship with outside world. Some apprehend whether we shall cease to be human altogether. Ronald Green, a bioethicist offers prospect of "Babies by design" by snipping and splicing the DNA in human eggs, sperm and embryos so as to fix faulty genes and adding genetic enhancements (*a la* genetically modified or GM cotton/maize). Today's science shapes up as tomorrow's challenges. Perhaps with a "status-quo bias", the opponents of genetic enhancements counter-argue that "the way things are is the best way they could be". At least for now, we remain stuck and aghast by the marvels of genetic engineering,

18. Economics as Solvent of Elders' Woes

Upto the level of middle-income, Manipur's elders have some sustenance [hedging] capacity themselves being mostly either pensioners or having earning dependents. But come the vast majority of poor, destitute and low elders belonging to the unorganized sector, old age pension of Rs 100, hardly ever is worth the salt. Elders are prepared to do whatever it takes to ultimately postpone death, and live contentedly. More so, as the idea that "life doesn't end at 60" is growing. Reverting to Manipur's 11,382 widows, divorcees, separated and never married persons (=3,314 males + 8,068 females in 1: 2.4 ratio) forming 0.52 per cent of total population (2001), it must be inferred that they have adapted wonderfully well, as if they possess an intuitive knack for survival without depending on others. Just like fish to water, they have all along taken to retail trade, supply-chain facilitators, and street-corner vendors, hawkers, and helpers in godowns etc in the two-millennia-old "Ima Market" of Imphal which used to be Manipuri female's exclusive preserve. Of late, male traders have infiltrated in the since-expanded second and third phases of the Imphal market complex. Yet female traders could face tough competition from males all these years with elephantine prowess, and magnanimity, rather than manage in their erstwhile rhythmic: "work-as-you-can-afford". For that matter, elderly separatees, divorcees, and never-married could as well re-marry, not for procreation but for their own easier survival and happiness – more than at "old age homes." Much for this very purpose, Mumbai matrimonial bureaus are finding 15-20 per cent more Mumbaikars of "above 55 years" currently registering. Further on, by any chance, can some well-disposed Manipuri widows, divorcees, separatees and never married females emulate Maharashtra in future as a self-redeeming measure for upkeep of "gender exclusivity" and "prolonged Alzheimer-free happiness"?

So far economics has been the greatest solvent of all social problems and geriatric challenges. Economics is taking over (*read* multi-tasking) society and culture by affording mechanistic design, cost-benefit analyses, mergers, acquisitions etc. In the new world order companies are the 'new government' even guiding society, shaping it with their 'products' and messages. Land, or other underutilized resources are getting fully utilized through privatization Special Economic Zones (SEZ). Desperate poor's 'future income' is being created through financial products (*read* pension) for rural/ unorganized sector labour by asking them (while still able-bodied) to co-contribute to pension fund. Poverty and unemployment are being overcome through rural employment guarantee and other means-enhancing schemes. Small and medium enterprises are being restructured, as is agriculture organized on business lines. Can this be a coming test of virtue for both the "economically worse-off elders" and "less-forthcoming youth"?

19. Tackling Elders' "Existential Compulsion"

Earlier the solution was "pay-as-you-go" system of financing pensions. Now today's workers pay for today's pensioners through the pension-fund mechanics – itself a huge liquid asset – while keeping their fingers crossed that a future generation of employees will jump up the taxes for their pensions. This works as there are many youth and few old adults. But "population ageing" is making it less and less affordable by gradually raising the ratio of pensioners to workers. It calls for a compulsive welfare-imperative (major) role of the State on par with elders' proud, unrepentant "existential compulsion", increasingly seen here. Hence an imperative to caution government leaders to handle old age concern as cases of "despair beyond despair"! If sons can't unburden basics of parental care; State can't disown its liability of rendering those extra (medicare, old age homes, etc).

That said, the right way to tackle population ageing is for people themselves to work longer and to save more. Reforms need also encourage to provide more for their retirement as they live longer by, not despairing but, redeeming themselves. They should not resuscitate old socialist pipe-dreams about "decommodifying" market economies.

NOTES

1. **Parenting**: Everyone loves a bargain; that's the essence of the virtual market-savvy counterpart of each and everyone. The choice-pattern while parenting may be twofold. The point of learning is that he wants to maximize his chances of both: surviving and reproducing. The son is wanted for a reason other than survival value. The elder has also a point of social display from an outstanding son or many sons – as true of minority communities out to bargain-hunt ethnic identity issues – just like a car makes its owner conspicuous. Deployed properly, he brings the rewards of his 'paternal status' and better 'mating' opportunities. Just like his predecessors showing their loves for their young ones or even in the animal kingdom, where things are no better. After he got what he wants from his son, he might in the process hit a "brick wall" for his son. For instance, he may fall in moneylenders' trap during son's careering, though as default – but certainly not a test case.

   Ultimately for all reproduction-survival conundrum to go on unabatedly, though, it helps if the displaying parent believes that he should beget a son. Truly having a loving son to marvel is something exclusive, which makes evolutionary sense-on and chain-transcendent. Yes, some unknown risks are involved as when the son turns out unworthy or just average. Parenting may be much more mundane and lowly, as per admissions of many a father. Yet it can be gainfully compared to high status activity *par excellence* like art collecting. The point of comparison is whether the former can be 'pretentious' as the latter is often alleged. But pretence may not be the true explanation for paying millions for a plain-coloured canvas with intrinsic qualities which he considers beautiful. Both have a gestation period which make up for the risk. Real worth of the son becomes known – as much as that of the canvas – only in the future. Time alone tells whether parenting would prove worthy, as much as the art collector whose painting may then cost a fortune.

Another point of comparison is that there is an art market, howsoever difficult it is to bring art-lovers together with painters on the same forum. The market mechanism provides a quick and effective way of learning what has helped others in the past and thus for allowing choices about what is nice and what is nasty to be made speedily and efficiently. This 'baby-booming' – sons' effort to replicate – may be so designated for its impact on the housing market and thereby on the US economy has been phenomenal but of late acting as a drag on China and India, so much so that the two emerging giant economies are trying to "decouple" from the America-led global meltdown. The end-point is that parenting has its direct impact via replication-effort or younger generation, who are far more thriving than the parents.

2. **Amish community**: Traditional Amish – old order Dutch communities in Pennsylvania, USA – have unusually old lifestyles compared to the fast American life. They continue to eat traditional food (abstain smoking, drinking, driving motor cars etc); stick to traditional farming and do not marry outside the community. And their males have same average lifespan as their females – 71 years. Interestingly, the team led by Dr Wen-Chi Hsueh of the University of California, San Francisco asked Amish volunteers to give blood samples. From these

they extracted DNA and measured the average length of the telomeres of all the 356 male volunteers and 551 female volunteers. Their findings are recorded in *Proceedings of the National Academy of Sciences*. Their finding is that telomeres of Amish men and women, adjusted for age, were of the same length. That positively correlates well with the fact that Amish males and females are equally long lived.

They apparently recommend by imputation that a healthy way of life is well known to prolong existence. But the best way to live a long life is to pick parents also, if at all possible. For they shockingly find that not only the length of telomeres of father correlates with those of daughters, but also same lifespan. Why the correlation wrinkles by showing up between father and daughter still remains a mystery. In a possible competition between father's gene and mother's gene inside the womb, it is still not clear though why some somas become more disposable. Biologists are "befuddled!"

3. **Manipur's 'ancestor worship' cult**: A son, bereaved upon loss of father, can live in a *make-believe world* that his deceased father is still chaperoning him with more than mere moral strength in his mundane affairs. An orphan may then feel *unscrambled* even in his rough and tumble, so the ancestor never casts him away even after death. Although not reversible, the dead can be deemed to inspire, transcend and help steer the survivor's boat in the sea of human woes. That is the soothing effect of *ancestor worship* – elevated to the status of a clan religion – and of the since-reinvented *living dead* theory on the bereaved souls. That's perhaps how the wise in ancient Manipur used to demystify the *riddle* or myth of life here and beyond. Without surprise, and to the credit of the then unique paternalistic society, such ancestral pontification extended to both genders – for now the surviving ancestor worship have since gained currency for both male and female progenitors. It also means, the descendents live virtually bedazelled with their perennial trust in their (dead) ancestors – whether living or dead. Hence there is little difference between *living dead* and *dead living* for the non-deads. So death would not haunt a survivor in Buddhist/Hindu societies.

APPENDIX: TABLES:

Table 1
Manipur Population (%) by Age-Groups (1911-2001)

Year	*Age-Groups*			*All*
	0-14	*15-59*	*60& above*	*Agegroups*
(1)	*(2)*	*(3)*	*(4)*	*(5)*
1911	43.5	52.3	4.2	100.0
1921	41.0	53.2	5.8	100.0
1931	42.6	52.5	4.9	100.0
1941	41.5	53.1	5.4	100.0
1951	40.3	53.6	6.1	100.0
1961	43.1	51.1	5.8	100.0
1971	42.5	51.4	6.1	100.0
1981	39.3	54.7	6.0	100.0
1991	35.2	57.7	6.1	100.0
2001*	32.6	60.5	6.9	100.0

Source: Economic Survey: Manipur 2007-08: Govt of Manipur: p.15
**Excludes Mao Maram, Paomata & Purul Subdivisions of Senapati district.*

Table 2
Comparative 60+ Population in 10 Age-Groups: Manipur (1991-2001)

Age-groups	*1991 Census*		*2001 Census*		*Difference*	
(1)	*(2)*	*(3)*	*(4)*	*(5)*	*6=(4-2)*	*7*
Total	Popn	%	Popn	%	Popn	%
60+	111,105	100.00	145, 470	100	34,365	100.00
Indices	100	-	131	-	-	-
60-69	69,612	62.63	84,030	57.76	14,418	41.96
Indices	100	-	121	-	-	-
70-79	29,614	26.68	44,265	30.43	14,651	42.63
Indices	100	-	150	-	-	-
80 & above	11,879	10.69	17,175	11.81	5,296	15.41
Indices	100	-	145	-	-	-

(Source: Census Reports)

Table 3
Above-60 Population by 5-year Age-Groups & Gender: Manipur (1991-2001)

Age-groups	1991 Census						2001 Census					
	Persons	*%*	*Male*	*%*	*Female*	*%*	*Persons*	*%*	*Male*	*%*	*Female*	*%*
(1)	*(2)*	*(3)*	*(4)*	*(5)*	*(6)*	*(7)*	*(8)*	*(9)*	*(10)*	*(11)*	*(12)*	*(13)*
60-64	43,709	2.38	23,632	2.52	20,077	2.23	48,133	2.22	24,343	2.22	23,790	2.22
65-69	25,903	1.41	14,221	1.52	11,682	1.30	35,897	1.66	17,990	1.64	17,907	1.67
70-74	19,705	1.07	10,576	1.13	9,129	1.02	28,806	1.33	14,561	1.33	14,245	1.33
75-79	9,909	0.53	5,090	0.54	4,819	0.54	15,459	0.71	7,894	0.72	7,565	0.71
80+	11,879	0.64	6,020	0.64	5,859	0.65	17,175	0.79	8,445	0.77	8,730	0.82
Total 60+	111,105	6.05	59,539	6.35	51,566	5.74	145,470	6.71	73,233	6.68	72,237	6.74
Total Popn	18,37,149	100	9,38,359	100	8,98,790	100	2,166,788	100	1,095,634	100	1,071,154	100

Source: Computed from official census records.

** Italicized figure in cols 3, 5, 7, 9, 11 & 13 are percentages to total population.*

Table 4
Centenarian Population of Manipur by Districts & Gender: 2001

State/ District	*Category*	*Persons*	*Male*	*Female*	*Ratio F/M*
(1)	*(2)*	*(3)*	*(4)*	*(5)*	*(6)*
Manipur	Total	162	54	108	2.00
	Rural	113	35	78	2.23
	Urban	49	19	30	1.58
Senapati	Total	6	2	4	2.00
	Rural	6	2	4	2.00
	Urban	-	-	-	-
Tamenglong	Total	8	2	6	3.00
	Rural	8	2	6	3.00
	Urban	-	-	-	-
Churachand-pur	Total	18	8	10	1.25
	Rural	18	8	10	1.25
	Urban	-	-	-	-
Bishnupur	Total	20	7	13	1.86
	Rural	12	5	7	1.40
	Urban	8	2	6	3.00
Thoubal	Total	29	7	22	3.14
	Rural	20	3	17	5.67
	Urban	9	4	5	1.25
Imphal West	Total	38	12	26	2.17
	Rural	13	1	12	12.00
	Urban	25	11	14	1.27
Imphal East	Total	26	8	18	2.25
	Rural	20	6	14	2.33
	Urban	6	2	4	2.00
Ukhrul	Total	10	6	4	0.67
	Rural	10	6	4	0.67
	Urban	-	-	-	-
Chandel	Total	7	2	5	2.50
	Rural	6	2	4	2.00
	Urban	1	0	1	Infinity

Source: Census Office, Manipur

Table 5
Districtwise 60+ Population of Manipur by 5-year Age-Groups (in %): 2001

Age-groups	*Manipur*	*Sena-Pati*	*Tame-nglong*	*CC-Pur*	*Bishnupur*	*Thoubal*	*Imphal West Total*	*Imphal West Urban*	*Imphal East Total*	*Imphal East Urban*	*Ukhrul*	*Chandel*
(1)	*(2)*	*(3)*	*(4)*	*(5)*	*(6)*	*(7)*	*(8)*	*(9)*	*(10)*	*(11)*	*(12)*	*(13)*
Total	100.00	100.00	100.00	100.00	100.00	100.00	100.00	100.00	100.00	100.00	100.00	100.00
0-59	93.09	94.49	93.46	93.65	92.16	93.30	92.09	91.28	92.96	92.63	93.51	94.22
60& above	6.71	5.37	5.71	6.15	7.42	6.60	7.73	8.57	6.88	7.22	6.36	5.72
of which:												
a) 55-59	2.22	2.02	1.92	2.18	2.36	2.18	2.41	2.58	2.23	2.18	2.08	2.13
b) 65-69	1.66	1.39	1.30	1.56	1.79	1.70	1.84	1.95	1.69	1.71	1.63	1.44
c) 70-74	1.33	0.97	1.07	1.17	1.49	1.31	1.59	1.82	1.39	1.50	1.29	1.04
d) 75-79	0.71	0.48	0.60	0.56	0.82	0.70	0.89	1.02	0.75	0.84	0.66	0.58
e) 80+	0.79	0.51	0.82	0.68	0.96	0.71	1.00	1.20	0.82	0.99	0.70	0.53
ANS	0.20	0.14	0.83	0.20	0.42	0.10	0.18	0.15	0.16	0.15	0.13	0.06

Source: Computed from: Report & Tables on Age: Series 15: Manipur : Census of India 2001

Notes: 1. Imphal West Urban Col No. 9 and 11 together make up Imphal Municipal Council population, showing markedly higher 60+ frequency.

2. ANS : Age not stated

Table 6

Districtwise Population of Manipur by Broad Age-groups: 2001

Group	*Person*	*Male*	*Female*	*(3-4)*
		MANIPUR		
(1)	*(2)*	*(3)*	*(4)*	*(5)*
All ages	2,166,788	1,095,634	1,071,154	24,480
0-14	706,705	360,867	345,838	15,029
15-59	1,310,080	659,114	650,966	8,148
60+	145,470	73,233	72,237	996
ANS	4,533	2,420	2,113	307
		SENAPATI DISTRICT		
All ages	156,513	80,230	76283	3,947
0-14	53,475	27,477	25,998	1,479
15-59	94,407	48,084	46,325	1,759
60+	8,417	4,557	3,858	699
ANS	214	112	102	10
		TAMENGLONG DISTRICT		
All ages	111,499	58,014	53,485	4,529
0-14	37,589	19,388	18,202	1,187
15-59	66,620	34,830	31,790	3,040
60+	6,363	3,295	3,068	227
ANS	927	501	426	75
		CHURACHANDPUR DISTRICT		
All ages	227,905	117,232	110,673	6,559
0-14	75,455	38,515	36,940	1,575
15-59	137,973	71,005	66,968	4,037

(Contd....)

(1)	(2)	(3)	(4)	(5)
60+	14,002	7,473	6,529	944
ANS	475	239	236	3
		BISHNUPUR DISTRICT		
All ages	208,368	104,550	103,818	732
0-14	67,814	34,685	33,129	1,556
15-59	124,257	61,701	62,556	(-) 855
60+	15,427	7,740	7,687	53
ANS	870	424	446	(-) 22
		THOUBAL DISTRICT		
All ages	364,140	182,250	181,890	360
0-14	128,471	65,450	63,021	2,429
15-59	211,287	104,581	106,706	(-) 2,125
60+	24,038	12,027	12,011	16
ANS	344	192	152	40
		IMPHAL WEST DISTRICT		
All ages	444,382	221,781	222,601	(-) 820
0-14	128,958	65,612	63,346	2,266
15-59	280,267	139,374	140,893	(-) 1,519
60+	34,342	16,340	18,002	(-) 1,662
ANS	815	455	360	95
Of which :		IMPHAL MUNICIPAL COUNCIL:		Urban Part
All ages	155,675	77,243	78,432	(-) 1,189
0-14	38,702	19,591	19,111	480
15-59	103,389	51,502	51,887	(-) 385
60+	13,351	6,010	7,341	(-) 1,331

(Contd....)

(1)	(2)	(3)	(4)	(5)
ANS	233	140	93	47
		IMPHAL EAST DISTRICT		
All ages	394,876	198,371	196,505	1,866
0-14	127,901	64,846	63,055	1,791
15-59	239,189	119,695	119,494	201
60+	27,153	13,478	13,675	(-) 197
ANS	633	352	281	71
Of which :	IMPHAL MUNICIPAL COUNCIL: Urban Part			
All ages	72,744	35,984	36,760	(-) 776
0-14	20,722	10,500	10,222	278
15-59	46,663	22,883	23,780	(-) 897
60+	5,249	2,531	2,718	(-) 187
ANS	110	70	40	30
		UKHRUL DISTRICT		
All ages	140,778	73,465	67,313	6,152
0-14	49,314	25,541	23,773	1,768
15-59	82,321	43,146	39,175	3,971
60+	8,960	4,666	4,294	372
ANS	183	112	71	41
		CHANDEL DISTRICT		
All ages	118,327	59,741	58,586	1,155
0-14	37,728	19,353	18,375	978
15-59	73,759	36,700	37,059	(-) 359
60+	6,768	3,655	3,113	542
ANS	72	33	39	(-) 6

Source: Report & Tables on Age: Series 15: Manipur: Census of India 2001
ANS: Age not stated

Table 7
Scheduled Caste (SC) Population: Manipur by Age-groups & Gender: 2001

Agegroup	*Person*	*Male*	*Female*	*Female-Male*
		MANIPUR		
(1)	*(2)*	*(3)*	*(4)*	*5=(3-4)*
All ages	60,037	29,934	30,103	(-) 169
0-14	18,878	9,591	9,287	304
15-59	36,760	18,177	18,583	(-) 406
60+	4,359	2,140	2,219	(-) 79
ANS	40	26	14	12

Source: Report & Tables on Age: Series 15: Manipur : Census of India 2001.
ANS: Age not stated

Table 8
Scheduled Tribe Population of Manipur by Age-groups & Gender: 2001

Age-group	*Person*	*Male*	*Female*	*Female-Male*
		MANIPUR		
(1)	*(2)*	*(3)*	*(4)*	*5=(3-4)*
All ages	741,141	374,319	366,822	7,497
0-14	250,615	128,534	122,081	6,453
15-59	443,970	221,278	222,692	(-) 1,414
60+	44,729	23,539	21,190	2,349
ANS	1,827	968	859	109

Source: Report & Tables on Age: Series 15: Manipur: Census of India 2001.
ANS: Age not stated

3

NUANCES ON THE ELDERLY PEOPLE AMONG THE TRIBES OF MANIPUR

Linus Neli[1]

Introduction

The people of Manipur are popularly classified into "valley people" (*tammi*) and "hill people" (*chingmi*)[2] largely due to anthropological reasons. The Meiteis, Bamons and the Pangals are the main inhabitants in the valleys, while the two generic groups of the Nagas and the Kuki-Chin Mizos populate the hills. In the Indian Constitution all the hill communities are recognized as Scheduled Tribes. The entire hill region has been divided into four administrative districts of Senapati, Ukhrul, Chandel, Tamenglong and Churachandpur and a semi-district area of Saitu Gamphazol. For over a hundred years, the majority of the hill people have embraced Christianity, but adhering to different Churches or denominations.[3] The original religion of the hill tribes is animism and it is survived even today by a few adherents from every tribe. Due to urbanization, many hill people have migrated to the valleys.

The scope of this paper is limited to the hill people and that, too, with reference to the scenario of the elderly people in the hills of Manipur. The paper is motivated by the fact that, the 21st century people are conscious of the well-being and the current slogan being: "Live long, live healthy, live wealthy, and live smart." We shall examine how much of this awareness has percolated into the tribal society in the context of Manipur.

The Elderly People in the Hills

It is difficult to ascertain the exact age of the elderly people among the hill tribes of Manipur, because decades ago most of their parents were either illiterate or they did not have the habit of recording the bio-data. Apart from the traditional birth ceremonies, there has been hardly any customary practice where the birth anniversaries have been celebrated. When asked about their age, these elderly people would begin with the phrase: "When the *Japan War* (i.e. WW II) broke out, I was already... looking after the cows, going to the fields...etc."[4] The Second World War had had a deep impact on the elderly people. They still have vivid memories of how the fighter crafts soared above their villages and bombarded their fields. They came into direct contact with the Allied Forces and the Japanese troops marching past their villages and slaughtering their pigs and chicken for 'fast-food' meals. Even today they have collections of the bombshells (some of which are now used as Church bells) and ruined arms and ammunitions. Depending on the descriptions of what they did at that time, one has to calculate their approximate age. It is rare to find people above 90 years of age, although there would be some claimants. There are more citizens who are between 70-80 years of age. Quite many of those who are enjoying service pension scheme today would be having their date of birth, but mostly fictitious. It is from among those who are about 50 years of age that would tell their chronological age accurately.

There is no yardstick to measure the commencement of old age. For a tribal man or woman, the old age begins as soon as some signs of physical disabilities begin to manifest. It would mean that their capacity to earn their daily livelihood has been impeded. Once an elderly person becomes weak and disabled, he or she becomes the most vulnerable person in the society, not only because he or she is considered a "non-productive" citizen but also such person has to depend intensively on the members of the nearest relatives and friends, and this is not always easy in the context of tribal economy, especially when it comes to expensive medical treatments.

It is noted that majority of the elderly people are women and, that too, widows are greater in number. The assumption is that most men have the habit of drinking and smoking. Moreover they consume a lot of salt water for stāmina and agility to work in the fields. This could explain for the short span of their lives. Besides, once their spouse had died, the widowers generally find themselves less capable to live single life for longer period than their counterpart. It is also observed that, thirty years ago, a person of 65 years of age would have died as an old man or woman. But the same age is not true among the present generation. The obvious reason being, the nature of occupation, social life, food and hygienic habit between the old and the present generation.

District-wise population and beneficiaries of old age pension scheme

Sl. No.	*Name of Districts*	*Population as on 2001 Census (provision)*	*Percentage of Population of the State*	*Number of Persons Registered for IGNOAPS**
	Valley Districts			
1.	Imphal West	4,39,532	18.40	5,317
2.	Imphal East	3,93,780	16.49	4,765
3.	Thoubal	3,66,341	15.34	4,433
4.	Bishnupur	2,05,907	8.62	2,491
	Total	14,05,560	58.85	17,006
	Hill Districts			
5.	Churachandpur	2,28,707	9.57	2,765
6.	Tamenglong	1,11,493	4.67	1,349
7.	Chandel	1,22,714	5.14	1,485
8.	Ukhrul	1,40,946	5.90	1,705
9.	Senapati	2,23,778	9.37	2,707
10.	Saitu Gamphazol	1,55,436	6.50	1,878
	Total	9,83,074	41.15	11,889
	Grand Total	23,88,634	100	28,895

*The *Indira Gandhi National Old Age Pension Scheme* (IGNOAPS) was launched on 19th November 2007. This scheme provides old aged people a sum of Rs. 200/- per month.[5]

Salient Features of Old Age Ailments

The common symptoms of old people are seen in terms of body aches in general, loss of hair, wrinkles, cataract, diabetes, prostrate enlargement, loss of memory, blurring of vision, bent shoulders, joint problems, spinal problems, respiratory problem, loss of teeth, impaired hearing, absent-mindedness, difficulty in controlling muscular power while attempting to go to toilets, faulty utterances of words and so on. There is no systematic care for old aged people in the villages. Some times it would look extraordinarily humane and dignified; while at other times so base and unearthly treatment would be accosted to them. It depended much on individuals and circumstances. Recently a villager reported that a woman aged 94 years was unbearably talkative and quarrelsome. Though old and weak, her tongue was sharper than any other tools in the village. For every act of love shown to her, she would reciprocate them in bitter words of blame and accusation. In the end those who did out of goodwill did not always succeed in treating her with care and compassion. Often the food was pushed to her as to a dog.

A peculiar problem of the aged people in the hills is the difficulty in ascending and descending the rugged terrain. The moment the hill people get old, their movement is very much curtailed to a tiny part of their village – at home. How else could they move – when there is no more breath, no more strength, and no more will-power? Automobile services do not exist in the interior villages. The only great desire they have is to visit their dear and near ones, to go to Church (normally built on top of the village not for any theological reason but purely for aesthetic view) and to go to the outskirt of the village for their habituated nature call.

Most of the villagers do not have access to television and radio with which to while away their leisure hours. Their only recreation is to see the grandchildren playing around them and narrate to them a folktale or two. At times such jolly hours would only end up in bad mood when the playful children tried to mimic their mannerism and disturbed their moments of peace and serenity. There is one more thing that the old aged people are missing in their villages, namely, the rhythm of the youth as most of them stay away from their villages in search of education and they would come home only during vacation.

A few decades ago, tribal women were socially tabooed to go to school, thinking that education would lead them to a life of promiscuity and bring shame and curse to the family and to the clan. Some communities never allowed the girls to grow long hair fearing that it would cause natural disasters upon the people and their crops. The female beauty was neglected because the paddy fields demanded intensive supply of labour. So much so the Meiteis have a saying: "It is better to marry a tribal girl than to buy two bulls to plough the fields." Today, these women are categorized as old aged citizens. After a long span of toil and suffering, they remain totally illiterate having paid the price of ignorance and superstitions. In their old age and ill health, and bent as they are at the sunset of their lives, they now deserve every respect and consideration as the unsung heroines of their respective tribe.

Regular Food Habit and Health Scenario

The regular food habit of the hill people consists of rice, meat (fresh or dried), fish (fresh or dried), edible insects (found mostly in paddy fields and in the woods), wild birds, vegetables (some are dried for Winter consumption); yam, pumpkins, potatoes, maize, millets, beans, etc (especially the items that can be preserved for long without refrigerators). They consume unadvisable amount of salt and hot pepper (*chillies*). The use of spices and edible oil is a recent phenomenon. A study conducted in Thailand and Philippine showed that edible insects were great suppliers of proteins and vitamins to the poor people who have no access to super market. Indisputably, this explains their subtle nourishments and contentment insofar as health is concerned. The hill people are also traditionally known for their exquisite rice beer. It contains high degree of starch and it is considered to be the principal food of the elderly people (if not banned by social disciplinary measures).

The elderly people have a galore of complaints about their sicknesses and ageing problems. When they are not able to enjoy the normal food, their health deteriorates fast. Medical resorts would be the last thing to do as that would invite financial problems. Interestingly, every tribe has some reservation of certain food items meant only for elderly people. These reserved items are associated with taboos, that is, implying with moral or physical punishment to the transgressor. To cite a few examples, the reserved items are: a) *domestic animals - brain* (a taboo that if eaten the children would get gray hair early), *testicles* (unmarried people would not be able to remain chaste); b) *birds* (certain birds would contaminate and make young people impure); c) *fish* (certain species of fish are not good for eyes, heart, etc), and d) *wild animals* (eating a wild cat meat would rouse evil temperament in young mind). The philosophy behind is not only to protect the young from harm, but also to reserve a reasonable share of precious food items for the elderly people. Undoubtedly, the young people would receive abundant blessings from the aged people if they brought such tabooed items as well as other general items when generously shared with their elderly people. Beneath the taboos and superstitions there is an underlying principle of mutual compassion, respect, care and support. These and many more values are embedded in tribal social traditions.

There are innumerable sayings of each tradition how to respect the elderly people; how to restrain from laughing at them, how to assist them at every place (especially splitting firewood, fetching water, blowing fire into flame for cooking and for warmth, etc). It merits a research on this topic itself.

Health Care Services

With the advent of education, health care services and interactions with the outside world, the health scenario has greatly changed, although not completely. In many villages the co-habitation of humans and cattle under the same roof has practically disappeared. Rearing of animals has become more hygienic and systematic. In almost every village we find some trained nurses, and in some villages even MBBS passed practitioners go round the villages. The elderly people in the villages are greatly receiving benefits from the improved accessibility to medical services. The popular catchword among the village folks is to administer a "vitamin-injection" to ailing old people. More often than not, the village nurse (trained) plays the role of a semi-doctor and pharmacist, besides being a nurse by profession. Since the villagers are mostly cultivators, they cannot afford to stay at home for days. The cultivators do not rest, because their works are never finished. They believe in the proverb: "Time and tide waits for none". The doctor's advice on "complete bed-rest" to the patients is never well received. Occasionally, the healers from outside Manipur like Assam, Burma and elsewhere used to visit the villages with herbal medicines, ointments, tablets, etc. Every tribe has its own therapeutic tradition – herbal, certain organs of animals, faith healing, witch-crafts, so many!

The geriatric medicines available to city dwellers have not reached a large area in the hills of Manipur due to lack of geriatric clinical centres. No one has ever done a diagnostic study of geriatric care in the hills. The establishment of such facilities would be costly and beyond the reach of the poor people. The senior citizens continue to feel neglected. Consequently, the number of depressed geriatric patients keeps on increasing.

The Role of the Christian Churches

The Christian idea of service is derived from the commandment of Jesus Christ: "Love the Lord your God with all your heart, with all your soul, with all your strength, and with all your mind; and love your neighbour as yourself".[6] A Christian, therefore, is not merely given the concept of service but actually called by God to respond personally and to take swift initiative in matter of service to the needy. This is a special mandate from Jesus Christ to his followers.

The introduction of Christianity brought a qualitative change in the tribal, inter-tribal, tribal-non-tribal relationship. To become a Christian meant to enter into a worldwide (Catholic or Universal) community and solidarity, following the dictum of Jesus Christ: "Love one another as I have loved you ... by this sign all will know that you are my disciples".[7] Through Christian missionaries, the tribal life, culture and tribal Churches came into direct contact with the international community.

The role of the Church or Churches in promoting health care and solidarity is expressed in a diversified manner. The Church as a community takes much pain to pay proper attention to the elderly people. Today, almost in every district, there are considerable number of Christian endeavours in running hospitals and dispensaries. There are also so called elders' forum, women society, youth organization, and other pious associations that cater to the needs of the elderly people.

Over and above the contribution of the Christian Churches, the call to humanitarian service is deeply embedded in the tribal traditions. The bonds of one family, one clan and one tribe have been the primordial ingredients of the tribal societies. The concern, care and support for the elderly people are part and parcel of their culture. The only regret being the lack of proper hygiene, dietary habits, poverty and lack of medical facilities that shorten the life span of the aged.

While living the healing mission of Jesus, the Christian Churches have made an immense contribution to the transformation of the tribal attitude towards health care. Homes for the orphans, the aged, and the handicapped have remarkably changed the situation of the poor and the marginalized among the tribal families. Such initiatives have reduced the anxieties of the elderly people whose children are assured of their future.

Some Practical Suggestions

As in any other societies, the urgent need among the tribal communities in the hills of Manipur is to create awareness as to how we can enhance the quality of life for the ageing people. Ageing is not a disease, but a process of realities that an individual is different from another. Ageing takes place within the context of friends, work associates, neighbours and family members. Here we shall concentrate only on two practical solutions:

1. **Active Ageing:** The term "active ageing" can be defined as a process of optimizing opportunities for health, participation and security in order to enhance quality of life as people age. It applies to both individuals and population groups. The principle of active ageing allows people to realize their potentials for continual participation in social, economic, cultural, spiritual and civic affairs, while providing them with adequate protection, security and care when they need. What the elderly people need is "minimum comfort and care". Older people who

retire from work, ill or live with disabilities can remain active contributors to their families, peers, communities and nations. They will learn how to age gracefully, knowing fully that gray-haired societies will not be a problem to any generation.

The combination of declining fertility and longer life spans has led to a surprising demographic development.[8] Keeping older folks employed is particularly important because by mid-century, says the U.N., the world will have more elderly people than children.[9] To compensate, several European nations have raised the retirement ages by as much as five years, while expanding anti-age-discrimination laws.

2. **Inter-generational solidarity**: One of the tenets of active ageing is the promotion of interdependence and intergenerational solidarity.

   In welfare societies, particularly in the West, senior citizens form themselves associations and clubs to live sociably, actively and meaningfully as they face the on-going process of ageing. The people in Manipur cannot afford the life-style of the welfare societies where there are so many forms of social securities and insurance policies. What we seek in our social context is to strive for a well-being (not welfare) society by establishing a sound network system of interdependence and intergenerational solidarity with the aims to extend healthy life expectancy and quality of life for all people as they age. For when they grow older we have to maintain their autonomy and dependence by reviving the traditional social values.

3. **Revival of the Village Elders' Council: A Remedy to Role Erosion:** The Council of the Village Elders is an institution held by elderly men who are renowned for their experience and wisdom. They render authoritative services to govern and promote the well-being of the whole community. They maintain diplomatic relation with other villages. They also act as agents of the chief as well as spokesmen of the community. The elders play vital influence and sometimes monitor the arbitrary actions of the village chief. For all these services, the elders receive no remuneration except the honour and respect they get from their village folks, although it is not always the case.

Today the role of the Elders' Council is getting eroded with the advent of post-modern culture imported from the cosmopolitan cities. It indicates a fast eroding process of the relevance of the elderly people in society, even if they have to live long. They are startled and bewildered by the intolerant and impatient attitude of the younger generation to bring about swift changes in society. What has gone wrong? It is like the iron getting rusty at a faster speed. The solution is to galvanize the metal with zinc to protect from rust. The truly and basically educated hill people should realize that, instead of dumping the traditional institutions and values into a thrash box, they could very well galvanize the gems of their traditional values with the help of science and technology from cultural pollution and develop their unique culture in a contextual manner so as to create a world of variety. This requires a collaborative effort of the old and the young, if at all there should be a continuity of the living tradition.

Conclusion

Today's senior citizens are different than their predecessors. They have to be more active if they have to live long, healthy, wealthy and with dignity and respect. It is our duty to maintain their lives and make them fit and agile with good health so that they can move in society decently and with dignity. Old people are facing increasingly vulnerable during and after humanitarian crises, due to their physical frailty and lack of mobility. They are abandoned as their children prefer to live separately after marriage or leave their places to make good of their career. Ageing is a challenge that cannot be addressed by the public or private sectors in isolation.

NOTES AND REFERENCES

10. The writer is a visiting professor at the Oriens Theological College, Shillong, and at the Institute of Oriental Canon Law, Dharmaram Vidya Kshetram, Bangalore. He is the Vicar General of the Roman Catholic Archdiocese of Imphal. He completed his Ph. D. (Rome) in ecclesiastical discipline connected with human rights. He belongs to Mao Naga tribe.

11. The nomenclatures "*chingmi*" (hill people) and "*tammi*" (valley people) are two Manipuri words which became popular since some centuries. Often they signify the contrasting difference between the two groups of people in terms of religion, culture, language, food habits, dress, methods of cultivation and governance, etc. The "chingmi" people basically come under the Indian Constitution recognized as Scheduled Tribes (ST), while the "tammi" people come under the General Race and

Scheduled Castes (SC). While there is no restriction for the hill people to come down and own land in the valleys, their counterparts from the valleys are not legally permitted to own land in the hills. Hence the study of demography will show significant difference in size, composition and distribution of population between the hills and the valleys.

12. Christianity was founded by Jesus Christ in the 1st century. Jesus Christ drew some followers and built up a believing community. This visible body of believers is known as the Church and is sustained by God, the Living Spirit. Christianity has its background from the Jewish tradition but eventually the new Christian way of life was opened to the whole world with the principal message to love God and one's neighbour. In course of time, due to socio-political reasons, the followers split up into churches (Catholic, Orthodox, Protestants) and denominations (divisions from among the Protestant groups which came into being during the Reformation period, and further leading to an ongoing reformulation of the concept of the Church).

13. The Battle of Kohima was fought between the British and Indian Forces and the Japanese Troops from April 4 to June 22, 1944 around the town of Kohima in Nagaland, India. Aftermath, the British and Indian Forces had lost around 4,000 men, dead, missing and wounded. The Japanese had lost more than 5,000 men in the Kohima area fighting. Cf. http://en.wikipedia.org/wiki/Battle_of_Kohima.

14. Due to the poor infrastructures, such benefits even though available are only a cause of disappointment and frustration to the villagers. They find it extremely difficult, if not impossible, to apply for such benefit as they or their proxy would have to go several times to the District Headquarter with photos and several documents for verification. The bottom line is, "Is it worth the trouble at all?"

15. See *The Gospel of Luke* 10:27; *The Gospel of Matthew* 22:34-40; *The Gospel of Mark* 12:28-31.

16. See *The Gospel of John* 13:34-35.

17. Whereas in the 1970s it was commonly said that by the 1990s

it was fashionable to argue that, for some developed nations, the opposite would soon be true. Soon, the argument went, there would not be enough able-bodied, young workers to support an infirm, gray-haired population.

18. By 2050, nearly a third of the developed world's labour force will be aged 50 or older, according to U.N. predictions.

4

CARE OF THE ELDERLY: A SOCIAL CONCERN

S. Saratkumar Sharma

Initially Elderly population is a problem of the West only not of the East. Stress and strain of modernisation, financial constraint, migration of population for employment, inadequate housing facilities in urban area, decline in the joint family system have made the position of the Elderly especially the sick and infirm vulnerable–both in developed and developing countries.

There are 7.66 crore elder persons in India as per 2001 Census (60 + above). Sex ratio among the 60+ is expected to rise as elder women will outnumber their male counterparts. Majority of them are in rural areas. By the year 2016, 51% of elderly population would be women.

The projected population aged 60+ and their percentage share in the total projected population as on 1st March, 2001-2026, as per the Report of the Technical Group on Population Projections constituted by the National Commission of Population, May, 2006, published by the Office of Registrar General, India is as under.

INDIA

Year	*Persons*	*% of persons to total population USA*	*% projected*
2001	70.69	6.90	
2006	83.58	7.50	
2011	98.47	8.30	14.00
2016	118.10	9.30	
2021	143.24	10.70	17.70
2026	84.62	12.40	21.80

USA:- At the turn of the century, life expectancy at birth in the United States was 47 years, compared with the more than 76-year life span projected for Americans born today. However, American working habits and life planning have not yet adapted to that increased life expectancy.

Indian Traditional Value System Respect

Elderly persons look after within the family, respected and honour, command their words, consultative status, children turn advice from the elders—considered an intrinsic part of the family.

i) Personal care, home and health care, social and recreational activities, emotional support, psychological support, informational support, instrumental support,

ii) Caring form elderly people, unlike caring for a normal child, involves everything dependency.

Constitution of India - Directive Principles recognises the care of the elderly. India is welfare State. Article 41 lays down that "The State shall within the limits of economic capacity and development make effective provision for securing the right to work, to education and to public assistance in cases of unemployment, old age, sickness and disablement and in other cases of underserved want". Additionally section 125 of the Criminal Procedure Code 1973 required every person having sufficient means to maintain his/her father or mother who are unable to maintain themselves. Similarly, section 20(3) of the Hindu Adoption and Maintenance Act enjoins on a person to maintain his or her aged and infirm parents.

In the joint family setting, elderly people are associating creative activities viz., story telling and share with the children, exciting time for the children, participate in the home work and outside the home, locality, community, ritual ceremonies. There was no superannuation and no retirement of age, elderly help these groups in the village, share their experience, their happiness and sorrow.

Present Changes of Pattern Exist

The present changing society is declining in status and opportunities to aged members which lead to comfortable, respectful and socially useful, neglected, unattended, helping hand, lack of care and protection from their children's, migrated to the cities, no one to look after them and also facing for financial difficulties, physical security, non recognition as useful and significant person, association and relation with the others, passing the laser time satisfactorily, increasing individualism widening generation gap, 2 or 3 generation to live together, acuate housing problem in the City, increasing employment of women outside the home, in offices, hospital, school etc. leaves very little time for the care of the aged. Socio-economic factors in rural areas lead isolation of aged by children.

Some of the research findings shows that "Old people living with their families have cordial living with their children and spouse, their social interaction are good in constrast to their counterparts living in institutions".

Government of India Initiative for Welfare Measures for Elderly

(i) Integrated programme for older persons (care, support to NGO – Old Age Homes, Day Care Centres, Mobile Medicare Units.)

(ii) Social Security mechanism for the poor older persons (Old Age Pension under National Old Age Pension Scheme, 1994).

(iii) National Policy for Older persons (NPOP) in 1999 (State support to Elderly for financial, food security, health care, shelter, protection against abuse, exploitation)

(iv) National Council for Older Persons (NCOP) (To advise Govt. policies and programmes and feed back, monitoring on implementation of the national Policy)

(v) Launched National Initiative on Care for Elderly (NICE) (Formulation and development of projects and training of personnel in the field of Old Age Care).

(vi) Celebration of International Day of Older Persons on 1st October every year.

(vii) Formulated Legislation to provide maintenance, care and protection to all persons and parents. "The Maintenance and Welfare of Parents and Senior Citizens Bill 2007" (statutory obligation, better medical facilities, setting up of old age homes in every District and institutionalization mechanism for protection of life and property of older persons).

Resource Utilisation Under Social Security Programme

In West - All Social Security including elderly programme accounts more than 30 p.c. of the total annual federal budget.

- By 2030, it may increase at 75 p.c.

In India - The amount earmarked in the Five Year Plans hardly touches the fringes of the problem.

State Programme

(i) Old Age pension @ Rs.100/- p.m. under State Scheme – 26,907 beneficiaries.

(ii) National Old age Pension @ Rs.200/- p.m. under Central Govt. – 43,619 beneficiaries

(iii) No. of Old Aged Home funded by the Govt. of India – 13 Nos. – 325 beneficiaries

(iv) No. of Day Care centres for Elderly — 14 Nos. - 700 beneficiaries.

(v) Annapurna scheme - 10 Kg of rice to the elderly people who are not covered under old age pension scheme.

For easing the problems of the aged :

i) Roles and relationship of older persons their families and community members need to be continually redefined as new groups to reach the age of 60 years.

ii) More governmental community support services for family care giving, more cooperative family care giving, more flexible employment practice.

iii) Old aged persons advantage of life long experience should be encouraged and utilised for the welfare of the disabled, schools, child care service, and also engaged them in various others social activities.

iv) Social support mechanism be provided to the aged to reduce physical and emotional strains to help them lead a healthy and happier old age.

v) Older retired people could be appointed as a teacher or mentors to teach some of their skill in local schools on a part time or volunteers basis. Elderly persons belonging to different professions having varied socio economic background may be engaged in community works for National development.

vi) Need based approach is essential. Besides covering basic and physical needs like food, shelter, clothing, necessary atmosphere should be created to fulfill other needs of the aged like, the need for companionship, recognition, the need for love and to belong, the need for esteem, and finally the need for self actualisation in the family.

vii) Universal Old Age Pension Scheme of all categories of Aged irrespective of income levels.

viii) Incentive for the sons/daughters to keep their elderly within the family,

- Rebate in income tax
- Provision of low interest housing loan
- Strengthening of domiciliary services including medical coverage looking after the elderly within the family.
- Day Care Centres for the Aged (Reduced burden of care and protection by the family)
- Compulsory old age insurance policy — Govt — Insurance Agency – Old people
- Few Hostel for the aged Institutional care
- More increase in family care setting.

- Opening of geriatric wards in Hospitals, separate queue for elderly persons in Hospitals and other public places (viz. Banks, Cinema hall etc.)
- Recreational Centre for elderly – providing recreation, craft activities, Gym, swimming pool, aged health clinic, transport facilities, canteen, conference hall etc. (for keeping the elderly cherful, active and healthy.
- Mobile Medical Care Unit for elderly.
- State policy for Aged and Plan of Action.
- Half way Home for the Aged.

"The aged no longer command respect as they used to because of an erosion of family values".

"The problems of the aged are manifold – financial, psychological, health, and social. There is an urgent need to ingegrate them into the family".

"The Global Community for the first time also expressed its concern in the World Assembly on Aging held in August, 1982 in Vienna - Launching of an International Plan of Action programme for economic and social security to older people".

"To-day's younger generation will become tomorrow's senior citizens what we do to our parents will be done to us in future. Let us realise that the seniors have sacrificed their life in building up our family and hence they have the right to retire and have a peaceful life when they are old. It should be our responsibility to see that members of our family are given due respect, love and care when they are in need".

Finally, elderly people should

* Considered as valuable cultural resources
* Role models for younger generation
* Motivate and create awareness among youths to take care of the aged in the family

Addison Joseph said:

" He who would pass his declining years with honour and comfort, should, when young consider that he may one day become old, and remember when he is old, that he has once been young"

TYPES OF SUPPORT	CAUSE OF FAMILY DISINTEGRATION	DISINTEGRATION OF FAMILY POVIDED BY FAMILY LEADS TO VARIOUS STRESSES AND STRAINS

(Urbanization,Industrialization, Migration, Social Mobility, Modern Values and Individualistic Outlook)

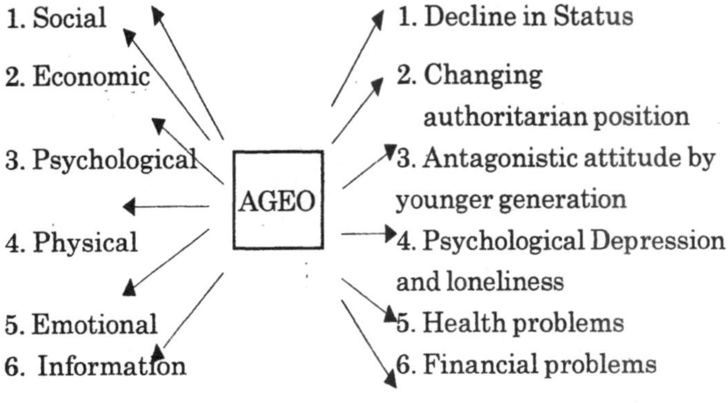

5

PSYCHO- SOCIAL ISSUES OF ELDERLY PERSONS

R.K. Lenin Singh

With medical advancement and improvement in living conditions people expect longer life span. However merely adding years to life is not the goal of our endeavour but the ideal should be adding life to years. General belief of old age is linked to loneliness, poor health, senility and general weakness and hence many people are afraid of ageing. For successful ageing, educational status of the individual, socio-economic status, are important factors. While we give more attention on physical factors such as exercise, diet, sleep, genetics etc, there is growing body of evidence that suggest that psychosocial and socio-economic factors also have significant influence on healthy ageing.

In Manipur, elderly people enjoy a special status. They are respected irrespective of their professional or social status. In any decision-making from petty matter to marriage, property deals etc the head of the family is usually consulted. In general, Manipur till today is an elderly friendly place. We respect people more by age (less by position) for instance, an officer addresses a peon as brother (if he is elder to him) and not by name. Elders are usually consulted before taking an important decision.

This article attempts to address some psycho-social issues related to ageing.

Retirement

Retirement brings a major change in the daily routine of individuals specially those who were actively involved in many activities. They have to adjust to their new schedule. If not prepared well ahead, most of the people find it very difficult and frustrating. They feel as if they have lost their status and authority in the society. Sometime they feel depressed and look rather older than their age.

Grief and Mourning

Many of the elderly have lost their spouse or siblings or relatives by their age. Death of a spouse is the most stressful event in one's life. They would miss their company, comfort and sometimes let go of their purpose of life. This might be the reason why many elderly persons die soon after the death of their spouse.

Empty Nester

Education and employment of their wards is the main concern of all parents. Their children grow up, mature, get employment and get married. After this satisfying moment many elderly persons have to stay back in their empty house all alone. There are many instances where all the children leave home because of their jobs or marriages, leaving behind their aged parents in the hands of helpers. Even for those who stay together in the same house their children are so busy and occupied in their own activities (official/job/business) and concern about their own children that they hardly spend time (quality time) with their aged parents. They miss their children and the past memorable days with them. Unlike in the past, these days the grandchildren are also too busy in their study, private tuitions (even they don't have time for play) etc. that the elderly persons are deprived of the pleasure of playing with them.

They have limited opportunity to meet their friends/ colleagues/relatives because of limited mobility due to physical ill health and lack of means.

Migration

Most of the successful businessmen, officials, contactors and professionals from rural areas migrate in the urban areas for reason of their official posting, convenience, comfort etc. They are happy and their children adapt very well in the new environment. But their aged parents, who have spent their precious life caring for them, would prefer to stay in their native place/home amongst the people they know and the environment they are accustomed to. They love the smell of paddy field, muddy roads, fresh air and the open field of the village life. They hate the concrete wall, noise and pollution of the urban set up. Moreover most of them prefer to die in the place where they were born.

The separation is very painful for the elderly persons who miss their children and grand children and in due course of time the gap (in terms of time and space) widens.

Nuclear Families

These days the concept of joint families is gradually loosing ground. Practically nuclear families are increasing in number in our state. In joint families there are many members of the family who stay together, help each other, and share their opinions, problems and achievements. In such families the elderly persons have something to contribute and when in need other members extend their support to them. In nuclear families where both the spouse work, there is hardly anyone to look after the elderly persons.

Let's pray and hope that the beautiful joint family system is preserved in the coming generations in Manipur.

Old Age Home

The need for day care centre and old age home arise these days as some of the elderly persons do not have any relatives or they refuse to take responsibilities for them (either they are incapable or unwilling).

Generation Gap

Today, there is a generation gap between the old and young. Most of the elderly people are not IT savvy and find it difficult to adjust to modern gadgets. On the other hand the young generations are crazy about the latest modern gadgets and cannot do without them. It creates a wider gap between the elderly persons and their children.

Lack of Recreational Facilities

There is no place/facility worth mentioning in Manipur where our senior citizens can have some recreation and relaxation. At home as there is no regular power supply home entertainment facilities such as television, video, radio etc cannot be utilized. It is definitely a torture to spend time without any recreational facilities.

Financial problem

Many of the elderly persons in our state do not have a regular income and are dependent on others. This is one of the important reasons for making a person discontented in old age.

Elderly abuse

It is not uncommon in Manipur that the elderly persons are neglected, ill treated, and even verbally and physically abused by their own children and relatives. Most of the time it remain unnoticed as the elderly persons have no opportunity/capability to complain. It is unfortunate that many of them live in pathetic condition and die like animals. The motive may either be to own their property or to relieve themselves off the burden of caring.

Law and order situation

The elderly persons in Manipur do not have peace of

mind because of the prevailing law and order situation. They always worry about their children who goes out for their duty/job/business till they come back home safely. The uncertainty of our society is always a source of stress for all.

Impact of HIV/AIDS

Manipur is one of the high prevalence states of HIV/AIDS in India. Many of the youths have been claimed by this disease. The norm is for the children to perform funeral rites for their parents but today it is observed that the aged parents are performing the funeral rites for their children who dies untimely because of their unhealthy behaviour. There are numbers of elderly persons looking after parentless grandchildren whose parents have died of this deadly disease in their prime time. This is a burden in the fag-end of their life and they cannot die peacefully.

Physical illness/problem

A nationwide survey conducted by the National Sample Survey Organization (NSSO) reported that 45% of the elderly suffered from chronic illness. Hypertension, coronary artery disease (CAD), diabetes, cancer, arthritis, dental problems, impairment of vision and hearing etc are common. Depression and anxiety are common among the patients suffering from CAD, diabetes and other chronic physical ailment. In some studies depression is found to be high as 17-27% amongst the hospitalized CAD patients and 24% amongst diabetic patients.

Mental Health Problem

Community study of geriatric population found a high prevalence of mental illness (34.9%). Depression is the most common disorder followed by dementia. Other disorders are functional psychosis organic brain syndrome, substance abuse and other neurotic illnesses. Depression is a condition in which one feels sad, tired and exhausted most of the time, suffer from loss of appetite, body aches, lack of interest in anything including enjoyable activities, feels restless, worthless and loses purpose of living and there is risk of suicide. Elderly persons, female sex, illiterate, widow, poor socio-economic status, poor family support are more prone to develop depression. But most of the time it may be considered as a part of ageing process and do not consider treatment.

When Memory is Fading (Dementia)

After the age of 60 years, forgetfulness and decline in overall cognitive function is observed in many of the elderly persons which will be increased proportionately with advancing age. It is known as Dementia. Alzheimer's disease is the commonest type of dementia followed by Vascular dementia. The prevalence of senile dementia is about 3.5% in the population above 60 years and it significantly increases as the population gradually grows old.

In the early stage, forgetfulness, difficulty in completing simple tasks e.g. everyday household chores and spatial disorientation are the common problems. Subsequently they become more confused, marked cognitive impairment and personality changes leading to odd behaviour, agitation, wandering tendency and sleep disturbance. In the terminal stage they become apathetic, doubly incontinent and bed ridden.

In such condition, one cannot look after oneself and in the advanced stage one is dependent even for the basic daily activities like toileting, food and personal care. One can imagine their anguish when there is no one to look after them in such situations. Dementia was construed as a normal part of ageing and was not perceived as requiring medical care. There is no effective treatment for this condition. But there might be significant improvement in some types of dementia e.g. Pseudo-dementia. This is a condition in which cognitive impairment is reversible and is mainly caused by depression.

Care givers of persons with dementia have to spent a significantly longer time in communicating/ supervising and helping with eating, personal care and toileting. They have marked economic strain to bear the increased healthcare costs, and many of them give up their job. Thus the rate of caregiver burnt out is very high and there is high chance that the care givers themselves might suffer from mental illness like depression.

Some authors like Don C. Blazer prefer the term Geriatric Syndrome to address the mental health problems of elderly people. The syndrome comprises of Acute confusion, Memory loss, Insommia, Anxiety, Suspiciousness, Depression and Hypochondriasis.

Conclusion

Quality of life in the elderly person is mainly affected by economic status, health status (Physical and mental) and social support systems.

In the past, old age was never seen as a social problem. Respect towards elders and the concept of obligation towards parents formed a part of the cultural value system. As in the joint family there was always someone to look after the elderly or the sick one.

But today because of several factors like urbanization, migration, the breaking up of joint family system, the changing role of women from being full-time home maker to full time job holder and increasing number of elderly in the population, caring the aged population poses a public health challenge.

It is time we should give a serious thought for our senior citizens, provide facilities for recreation, socialization, give priority in public places like public transport system, bank etc, provide re-employment facilities so as to let them have a meaningful healthy ageing.

Super specialities like geriatric medicine and geriatric psychiatry should be developed and all the health care providers should be sensitized about the specific issues of elderly persons.

There goes a saying, "What goes around, comes around". So, we should treat others as we would treat ourselves or that we could like to be treated.

In framing Government policy for the aged people psycho-social issues should also be given priority.

6

THE ELDERLY – WOES AND INTERVENTIONS

S. Kunjabihari Singh

Introduction

Years back, sometime in June 1998, in New Delhi's Satya Marg, a posh residential area, I was invited to lunch by a couple-friend of mine. Both belonged to the IAS and had two children. At lunchtime, an elderly person, tall and lanky meekly joined us; he turned out to be my friend's father from a village in Bihar. The mother tried to sooth her two children not happy with the food prepared hurriedly by their mother, in the absence of the domestic help, on leave. Their grandfather, on a brief visit, apparently could not manage enough courage to look at them, let alone trying to pamper or cajole with the lovely grandchildren, as normally should happen. He quietly savoured his allotted food, without attracting any care and concern from either of the couple. The old man hastily collected bowls, the plate, picked up the few rice incidentally dropped on the table, and hurriedly left for the kitchen. To my surprise, the couple, his own son and daughter-in-law didn't, I repeat, didn't think it worthwhile to stop him from lifting the plate. The old father, must have, to be sure, cut short his stay with his IAS son, to be back to his village-house, to find some minimum dignity and somebody to talk to and someone to keep company, so dear to his heart, if not good food to eat or nice place to stay. He must have preferred to face the embarrassment, he had to encounter back home, on returning so soon rather than face isolation, day in, day out, in the house of his son.

Shri Daljit Singh and *Smt. Swarn Mongia*, now in the eighties, had three daughters who all migrated to the US. For 10 years, the elderly couple, green card holders, found solace in shuttling between Delhi and the U.S. sharing time with daughters, sons-in-law and the grandchildren. So far so good. In April, 2007, however, the couple felt they had enough of pilgrimage; surrendered their green cards, disposed off their flat in posh Panchasheel Park. This was not the end. They choose to stay put in an Old Age Home in Dwarka. They justified "while in Panchasheel Park and more so in the US, they had hardly any companion, they got a plenty of it now in the Old-Age Home."

Shrimati Y. Bimola Devi, in her late fifties, is teaching in a government primary school. She lives with her husband a retiree, with the only son and daughter-in-law. The young couple are unemployed. Bimola and husband had to face the ignominy of regular abuse and humiliation from the only son who even slapped her one day–reason–the parents have failed to make a man out of the son and they are responsible for all the woes the young couple encounter. The elderly father had, under duress, to sign an authority letter to share 50% of his paltry pension with his unemployed son. The young daughter-in-law rather than dissuade her husband from abusing the parents lent support to her husband. Bimola is looking earnestly for an alternative place to stay, yearning for some respect, some love, which they so richly deserve, at their age.

The above are only a tip of the iceberg of varying scale and magnitude of elderly-abuse; more daunting cases are swept below the carpet for fear of embarrassment and disgrace in an open society. In the resulting scenario, only the elderly who so dearly seek some solace end up being abused and abandoned.

2. Magnitude of the Problem

Members of generation born between 1948-1958, are fast approaching 60 and above years. Already there are those born before 1948, in the elderly club. In India elderly person is estimated to constitute about 7% in 2001 and is projected to rise to around 10% by 2021. Population of 60+ age group is estimated to rank 4th highest in the world. In Manipur the position is equally alarming—around 7% or roughly 1.7 lacs population constitute 60+ in 2007. In another 20 years, additional 10% would join the grey club. Considering the decreasing death rate from to during 1993 to 2003 and increase in longevity with rise of life expectancy to around 60-65, the population of the elderly person would constitute alarming proportions by 2020.

3. Attributes to the Problem

With the ultra-modern life styles holding the sway, where both husband and wife go out for working, quite a few, staying outside and abroad, in search of greener pastures, coupled with increasing lure for divided/ separate families, today, the elderly parents are deprived, ignored and alienated a lot. The sons and daughters-in-law of today with their high profile taste of privacy and personal choice prefer the elderly to remain shut to their domain; and stubbornly refrain from keeping the parents into confidence in family and social matters. An opinion poll conducted by Times of India sometime ago about the changing life styles of the modern couples vis-à-vis the elderly, the elderly parents desperately long for some importance attached to them in family matters while the majority of the daughters-in-law expect the parents-in-laws to keep away from these matters and that they rest satisfied with the shelter given and food provided.

This way, the traditional grand, joint-family-system where the sons and daughters-in-law stayed together, with their parents, where the kids with their usual noise and laughter squabble to entice the grand parents in the evening for this fable or that, is swept to the way-side and is more of a story of the past generation then a reality today. With modernity kicking in, the elderly has been marginalized more than even before. In the result, despite having a shelter and provision for food sizeable proportion of them started feeling the pains of isolations and alienation in the land of theirs. This ground reality is itself painful disease for these seniors.

The state of Manipur has fortunately an open society with a strong social bond. The families are conscious of the possible social gaze and condemnation, in the event of such an act of alienation. And yet, with swings of change setting in gradually, though slowly, the issue of elderly-care has assumed such magnitude of importance and urgency than even before.

4. The Grey Blues

A conservative estimate puts 60+ population growing at 38% vis-à-vis 19% of the rest of the population. This high dependency-ratio is itself a cause for concern. Coupled with this is the fact that around 33 to 37% of the elderly are projected as economically dependant. 40% are without a spouse-an irreparable loss at their age. Plus, in a fast-changing scenario in a dynamic family-fabric, many of the parents are left alone, if not truly abandoned by their children. The traditional values, social status and reliance on the elderly are fast loosing ground. The pang of isolation, loneliness is increasingly felt without much ray of hope for improvement. In addition, apart from social illness like abuse and humiliation from their own children, the geriatric illness that invariable have to set (in a situation where they are more isolated than not) are the worst fears of the grey-club.

High economic dependence of the elderly is another grey area. At a time where the economically well-off elders are complaining about lack of emotional support, worst still, abuse and humiliation, the plight of the economically dependent elders is understandable. Isolation and loneliness, lack of social and economic activities ate other factors to make the elderly feel alienated and uncared for.

5. What Do We Do

Evolving suitable measures to ease the many forms of woes of the elderly, let alone eradicating the same is, by itself, a complex proposition, There cannot be quick fix solution; the problem- an offshoot of the advent of modernity, has only to be attempted to be lessened in scale and magnitude. Two approaches, inter-alia, can be thought of.

One is institutional-where public package, schemes, often in the form of welfare measures and facilities in public establishments are doled out increasingly. There could be instituitionalisation of instruments for social and also economic security of the elderly. Like, for instance, the National Policy for Older Persons framed by the Government of Indian in Jan., 1999 with the objective for taking special care of and provide protective measures to the senior citizens. There is also National Council for Older Persons constituted by the Centre to aid, advise and operationalise the National Policy. The need of the hour is, however, to activate these institutional mechanisms. The recently announced national programme for the elderly with a staggering outlay of Rs. 400 cr., the setting up of two national Institutes of Ageing, with eight Regional Institutes; opening of separate Department of Geriatric Health Care in one Medical College/Hospital in each state are positive steps. Similarly, the schemes of health insurance for the elderly, coverage of 60+ age group for the old-age pensions; the reverse mortgage system empowering the elderly owning some property to mortgage the same from financial institutions etc., certainly enhance opportunities for these categories of the people.

The important issue is, however, the effective implementation of these schemes. Given the kind of relatively humble status, the elders are placed today how many of the eligible parents would be bold enough to go for the reverse mortgage system, so long their children in some cases, the spouses, do not fall in line. Then again the scheme of old age pension covering 60+ age group. Under the existing scenario, wouldn't majority of the eligible persons end up being denied any benefit, leaving it to a handful of them having some connection considering again the usual excuse of constraint of resources.

Having briefly discussed the institutional approach we can think of another one where the strategy largely builds on providing physical infrastructure. These may be of immense relief for the majority of the elderly who do not have any one to fall back, physically and financially even otherwise. They are not rich enough to reap the benefit of the institutional facilities, nor do they have children to lean upon. There is plenty of such no-so-fortunate elders in our midst. We have, as a civic society, the obligation for providing them a relatively peaceful place at this stage of their life's journey, where they do not suffer from abuse, intimidation, and worst still, the dreadful glare of the in-laws and where they have somebody to share their woes and happiness, however little that might have left in store. The Government of India, Ministry of Social Justice and Empowerment, provides funds to the extent of 50% of the capital expenses on raising Old-age Home and 90% of the revenue expenses for running the home. Oddly, not many takers are there. More and more civic organizations should come up to take up such homes but the effort calls for tremendous amount of labour and sacrifice. Such homes should be able to provide necessary fillip, the kind of platform, where they can start a life of near – normal existence. It is these homes, the likes of the Mongias, the Nandas, the Bimolas need, a home out of their own homes, where they can breathe peace, can think of some solace, feel the bliss of some care and get some company to slowly bury the past into oblivion and can help in restoring a faint smile back to their lips. These should, at least, deserve this much privilege on the eve of their departure from amidst us.

For pensioners, the system of disbursement need further streamlining. Citizens' groups and neighboring committees empowered to meet the appropriate authority for grievances would be ideal. Such bodies have greater role in case of the non-pensioners but getting benefit of old-age pension, particularly where the coverage of eligible elders is a suspect.

Adequate motivation to step up Senior Citizens' Club to provide opportunities for recreation, company, gossip, reading etc. would be a food for thought. Such clubs could take care of health and related problems of the more vulnerable age-groups. The more able, educated senior citizens could be tapped to help in propagating literacy programmes, in community, religions and social activities.

Old age homes for dependent seniors who do not have anybody to support, financially or otherwise, are indispensably required. Even for those economically independent and despite having a home to stay but not finding solace in their own homes, could be covered under the above. The government encourages setting up of such homes by giving 50% grants for construction and 90% grants for recurring expenditures. Nevertheless, the takers are quite few and far between. In this respect, the All Manipur Senior Citizens' Welfare Association, Manipur has constructed one Old Age Home and is in advanced stage of completion. We can only sum up by saying that the critical dependence of the aged on state or society be not lost sight of the minimum dignity.

REFERENCES

1. Harsh Mander and Vidya Rao (1999). *An Agenda for Aging Interventions and Marginalised Groups,* Voluntary Health Association of India, New Delhi.
2. Jacquelyn Lynn and Charlene (2006). *Davis Senior Services Business,* Entrepreneur: Canada.
3. *Statistical Abstract, Manipur 2005,* Directorate of Economics and Statistics, Govt. of Manipur.
4. *India Today,* July 2007.

7

THE GENERAL HEALTH CONDITION AND ACCESS TO HEALTH CARE SERVICE OF THE OLD AGED PEOPLE

Th. Achouba Singh

Aging is a natural continual process beginning with birth and ending with death. Once we are born, one day we are to die. This journey of the life which passes through different natural sequential milestones is a fixed one. No one can modify it. Everyone of us is to grow older and older day by day till we reach the last stage of life, death die to old age. Human beings may be able to survive upto a maximum age of 150 years (genetic theory). Till date few individuals have reached upto 125 years (in the record). If we can control maximally the factors which injures and harms us and can improve maximally the factors which favours us in our survival many more individuals may be able to cross the age of 130 and also 140.

But, literally those who cross 60 years are considered as old aged. This may be acceptable from many views. That, by 60+ years many retiring from services, many are physically, mentally, economically and psychosocially dependent on others i.e. mainly on the youths of the family and society. As they are deprived of many basic needs of the life, their life tend to step into a miserable and horrible journey. But, this journey is for all. Everyone of us to pass through and to end there itself. Knowing and understanding for this fact, we better and surely have to prepare the best pavement for the unavoidable journey by using and consulting all the possible helps. We should make the last journey a very comfortable one so that everybody is attracted to that and gets the most respectable and dignified life status.

The spectrum of the general health conditions of the old aged people are many and varied differing from place to place, community t community and country to country.

In Indian context, the major health problems are as follows [Major Morbidities (ICMR, 1980)].

- Visual impairment - 88.00%
- Locomotive disabilities - 40.00%
- Neurological diseases - 18.70%
- Cardiovascular diseases - 17.40%
- Respiratory diseases - 16.10%

- Skin diseases 13.30%

Major Morbidities (recent)

- Hypertension -39.53%
- Cataract -35.30%
- Arthritis -33.67%
- COPD (chronic obstructive pulmonary diseases) - 19.92%
- CHD (coronary heart diseases) - 18.85%
- Benign hypertrophy of prostate - 16.23%
- Diabetes Mellitus - 15.23%
- Irritable bowl syndrome - 09.20%
- Depression - 08.50%

Some of the major health problems in the north-Eastern Region are:

- Joint pain/ache
- Cataract
- Peptic ulcer
- Dysentery
- Urinary problems
- Asthma
- Diabetes
- Hearing problems
- Hypertension

- Giddiness
- Constipation
- Toothache

The access to health care services

The cares can be given by any of the following individuals/organizations/bodies.

- Government
- NGOs
- Civil societies
- Individuals
- Families
- Social workers
- Academic organizations
- Religious organizations

The main problems including the health ones are

- Health Care
- Shelter
- Nutrition
- Psychological Problems
- Loneliness
- Family separation
- Non-availability of opportunities such as doctors, nurses, hospitals, nursing homes
- Socio-economics concerns.

■■■

INDEX

■■■